Wells for Shepherds

An Anthology of reimagined and retold Bible stories and truths

"The land by the sea will become pastures having wells for shepherds and pens for flocks."
Zephaniah 2:6

Hetty Stok

Extra material Jacqui Stok

Illustrations Jeanette Stok

Copyright © 2023 Hetty Stok

Email: hettystk@gmail.com

ISBN   978-0-6457204-0-2

To my special bunch of crazies:

Pieter, Nut, Kik, Jac, Al, Caz, Aaron, Rosey and Paul.

And the next generation who take crazy to another level:

Teddy, Beth and Meg.

This book is for you, with love.

Table of Contents

Foreword

Introduction

Telling Bible Stories to Young children	1
Bible Black Holes	3
David	5
David and Jonathan – Friends	9
Ellie and the Pretend Snake	13
God is my Maker	17
The Littlest Disciple	21
Encountering Jesus	25
Time for Revenge	27
Sophia's Pictures	31
Feeding of the 5000	37
God takes the Shakes Away	41
"Samuel, Answer to my Prayer"	45
Saul on the Road to Damascus	51
Hiding	57
I've Heard about Jesus…	61
The Conscript	63
Jesus Clears the Temple	67
Honesty	69

A Child in their Midst	73
Melchior, Balthazar, and Caspar	77
Mud – the Story of Jeremiah	83
Noodle in a Haystack	87
Old Martha	95
The Weeniest, Teeniest Seed	99
Rachel's Lamb	103
Stephanie's in Heaven	107
Nice	109
Story for Rohan	113
The Invisible Man	117
Stargazing	119
The Parable of the Lost Lego Block	123
The Man on the Ground	127
The Wedding at Cana	131
Put a Smile on God's Face	133
Tom's Fishing Lesson	137
Is God Grumpy?	143
Two Chippies	147
Do You Recognise Me?	151
Joshua	155
The Baby in the Hay	163

The Big Adventure	167
Eliab, The Boy Who Couldn't Be Still	177
Index of Bible References	181

Foreword

Hetty was involved in children's ministry for many years. Her passion to see children and children's ministry leaders grow in their faith was always her foremost goal. Her programs and lessons, as well as her mentoring of the teaching team, were infused with dynamic creativity which is evident in this anthology.

This book exemplifies her passion, containing stories for all ages. It encourages readers and listeners to sit up and wonder anew about the Bible and its timeless message. She has the special gift of seeing the 'other' – the bystander, the young child or the forgotten face in the crowd, and then introducing us to their questions and observations.

Above all, 'Wells for Shepherds' is an intergenerational resource. The book is born out of a strong belief that a Christian community, including worship, should be intergenerational – not segmented. Therefore, 'Wells for Shepherds' is a book for all ages. For the old to read to the young or to read for themselves. For young and old to explore together the textures and nuances of Scripture. In the words of 'Godly Play' the book's aim is to generate wonder in all ages.

'Wells for Shepherds' is an anthology of over 40 stories (including a picture story), plays and poems inspired by the Old and New Testaments. It can be used for personal reading, group discussions, children's classes – and hopefully, mostly, where generations meet together.

Pieter Stok

January 2023

Introduction

My favourite word is 'why'. It's also a favourite word of most children, as every parent will know in the frustration of trying to answer their child's endless chorus of 'whys'.

'Why' doesn't necessarily require an answer. It's often said when the world around us is confusing. It sharpens our senses to possibilities.

So when I engage with a Bible passage I make an attempt to put a child in it; a child who is giving the events a dose of 'why'. And occasionally it's an old woman or a bewildered pig-herder who utters that word.

Come along … sit beside Simon under the tax collector's table, lie on the sand while Sophia sketches, stand among the camels with Ellie. The questions may not be answered but the Spirit of the universe will bless the inquirer with new insight.

Of course, this doesn't mean the content of this anthology is only for children. The church has sheep of all ages, and my hope is that the stories will be like wells for shepherds: parents, teachers, pastors, brothers and sisters.

As I reflect and write of the stories in the Bible, the characters take on the personalities of people I've known. And along with them comes some modern-day props. Hence, it is difficult to write a boy from my Sunday School class into a first century Palestinian town without putting a beaker of cold lemonade in his hands. And how could my three wise men find a star without peering through a telescope? My stories are about real people, imagined people, and occasionally imagined people in real historical times and places.

Mo, Lizzie, Zoe and Benny were puppets made and operated by a willing group of 14 and 15 year-olds. As part of the Sunday School curriculum I developed, these scripts helped our team of young puppeteers bring another dimension of storytelling for the younger children.

There are only two 'Pelican Pip' stories here, despite writing hundreds of letters under that pseudonym for the children of our country church. Each letter was delivered weekly and contained a brief paragraph to illuminate the essence of that week's sermon. Pip's fishing lesson for Tom gives some insight into who Pelican Pip is and what's important to him. 'A Big Adventure' imagines Pip's interaction with his human friends; a loving and caring postman-intercessor who loves fish.

Finally, thank you Jacqui for allowing me to include your poems; true examples of your amazing creativity, originally written for our 'Kingdom Kids'. Also, thanks to Nut, our gifted artist, and Pieter whose patience as 'publisher' never ran out.

Hetty Stok

January, 2023

Telling Bible Stories to Young children

The story of Jesus washing His disciples' feet. (John 13:1-17)

Often those who tell Bible stories try to interpret the stories. We want to be sure the child understands the meaning and the lesson. In short, we tell the child what they should think. I'm wary of this approach.

I believe that when we impart God's Word to young people, when we share a portion of Scripture with them, the Holy Spirit is present and active in their hearts and their heads. We need to trust that He will guide them as they hear our stories. Our aim should be to facilitate worship in children.

So, how could we tell *this story* of Jesus washing the feet of his disciples?

Traditionally, we concentrate on Jesus, the teacher, humbling himself to minister to his friends. There is an understanding that Jesus is the important one, his disciples less so. Therefore, the Saviour is inverting a common practice.

However, to a child, this would not seem unusual at all. Their experience is normally one of adults caring for them - teachers and childcare providers, parents, and grandparents. It would be strange to them if the disciples had washed Jesus' feet! Keep this in mind.

The lives of children are full of friends, family gatherings, travelling, food, and identity. This story has it all. Jesus plans a meal together with his friends. They all travel to an upstairs room in a house. They probably walked along dusty roads to get there. When they arrived there were probably hugs and kisses all around. The table had an array of food and drink, lovingly prepared by others in their faith family. Most importantly, Jesus was with his friends: they identified themselves (and the community recognised them) as His followers. So, as you tell this wonderful story, touch on these points of contact. Because children will also visualise the story as you tell it. They will 'see' it, using their own experiences. For example, a table full of food will be their family's dining table.

Enrich the story for them by describing the colours, the smells, the icky-ness of the dirty feet, the warmth of the water in the basin, the gentleness of Jesus' hands, and the softness of the towel.

When we tell stories in this fashion, we help a child take it into their heart. The story will resonate with them.

And finally, give the child a way to respond to what they have heard. Wonder with them, sit quietly and ponder, provide art materials, sing. Follow their lead as they follow the Holy Spirit.

Bible Black Holes

Did you know there are black holes in the Bible? There are mud puddles, canyons, and prickle bushes as well.

I know about these because I tell Bible stories to kids.

Have you ever noticed how many empty spaces there are in Bible stories? For instance, what did Jesus and Zacchaeus discuss over lunch? And what was happening on Easter Saturday?

Try telling these stories to children. They're not afraid of black holes. They will launch straight into them. Slimy mud puddles that most Sunday school teachers avoid, such as how Mary got pregnant? Kids will take a running leap into that one. Tricky prickle bushes that college theologians won't venture near. No problem for the minds of five-year-olds. Three brothers of preschool age once explained the Resurrection to me.

Grownups can read the signs at the top of an 'exegesis' cliff that say, 'Don't go too close to the edge' or 'Danger Unstable Cliff Edge', but kids only see an opportunity to explore. Burning bushes, talking donkeys, floating zoos, miracles.

And the best part is that they will joyfully take the grownups by the hand, if we are willing to let them lead us.

Next time you're reading your Bible and you find a black hole, find a child to tell the story to. Sit alongside them and wonder together. No space suits, flack jackets, parachutes, or safety harnesses required.

David

A retelling of 1 Samuel 16: 1-13

The row of ants marched across the warm rock. The lead ant paused to take in the antics of a ladybug that the troop was about to pass. Every ant in the line momentarily stopped also, as it passed the bigger insect.

Taking his eyes off the ants, David mused, then he rolled over onto his back. He squinted at the bright afternoon light. He could see, far off near the eastern edge of a clear blue sky, the almost full moon. *How far was it?* David thought. *How many days' walk to reach the moon, if a boy could walk across the sky? What would that distance look like across the palm of Yahweh's hand?*

David sat up. He could hear someone calling his name. He stood and scanned the valley below. All his sheep - his father's sheep - were grazing on the summer pasture. Beyond them a figure appeared and David recognised Abel, his family's servant. He picked up the shepherds' crook and his lyre and bounded off, past the sheep who momentarily stopped, not unlike the ants, to watch the boy rush between them.

"Abel, why have you come?" he asked the old man. "Has something happened at home?"

"Shalom," replied the servant. "Your father has sent for you. Go. I will stay with the flock until you return."

David glanced at the crook and the lyre in his hands. He hesitated before handing the crook to Abel. Then he thrust the lyre towards the man as well. "Play for them. They love it." Abel grinned.

The boy-shepherd turned and ran down to the homestead.

Before David got to his home another servant met him.

"Is my father ill?" he asked the man.

"No, he and your brothers are with the Prophet. They are making sacrifices to the LORD."

"What has this to do with me?" asked David.

By now they were at the well in the courtyard.

"Wash your face and hands and put on these clean clothes."

David's mother then appeared. She took the cloth from the servant and began scrubbing at David's neck, tutting about the grass and gravel smudges on his face and arms. Her son was taller than her now, so she had to pull his head down to reach. The boy tried to get out of her grasp.

"Mother, what is going on?" He pleaded.

But there was no time for answers. Soon enough David was escorted into Bethlehem and then told to go to the place where his father and seven older brothers were standing. Another man was also there - the Prophet Samuel.

David could tell that his brothers were restless. Eliab, tall and strong, was the oldest, and he glowered when he saw the littlest of his brothers come tearing around the corner towards them. The boy-shepherd skidded to a halt a few yards from the group, took a deep breath, and calmly walked the final distance to stand before his father.

If I could run to the moon, he thought, *I could get there sooner.*

Jesse put his hands on David's shoulders and forced him to pivot around to face Samuel. The Prophet seemed not to notice him; he was in a deep reverie.

"Your servant, David, Jesse's son," David said, and he bowed. The Prophet was not physically tall. He was a full head-height shorter than the boy-shepherd. But David felt as if he was bowing before a someone of giant importance. He felt ant sized.

Something - not his father's hands this time- compelled David to kneel.

And then … and then, something amazing happened. The Prophet held a ram's horn of spice-infused oil above the head of Jesse's youngest son, as the other seven sons looked on, and he upturned the horn. Samuel proclaimed that David was the next King of Israel, anointed by YAHWEH!

As the oil came first on his head and next dribbled down his neck and into his shirt, David took a sharp intake of breath. He held the fragrant air in his chest, unable to decide if there was something different about him. Unsure if this meant he should or could still be himself. Unsure if breathing was necessary.

His father and brothers came forward and, one by one, embraced him.

"Now let's eat!" The Prophet declared loudly.

As the sun began to sink into the horizon, the shepherd-king tramped across the valley towards the sheepfold. Abel stood in the opening. "They're all in there, present and accounted for," he said. "And you're right. They do love the music of the lyre."

David drew his woollen cloak around himself and squatted in the opening as Abel started back in the direction that David had come. Some of the ewes nuzzled against him, sniffing at the strange scent of the anointing oil.

Not twenty yards away the old servant turned and shouted at him, lifting a thumb towards the sky:

"Full moon tonight!"

David and Jonathan – Friends

A puppet play for Mo and Lizzie

Mo: Friends, Friends, Friends! Who needs friends?

Lizzie: You having troubles, Mo?

Mo: You betcha! Lizzie, I'll be glad if you're the only friend I ever have.

Lizzie: I'm pleased about that Mo. But how come you're not going to be friends with anyone else?

Mo: They always let you down, you know.

They are useless, unreliable, unpredictable, and just annoying.

Take my EX FRIEND Jerry. He promised to be on the corner this morning with last night's homework. Was he there? NO! So Miss Turner gave me lines because I didn't do my homework.

Like I said. USELESS, UNRELIABLE AND ANNOYING!

Lizzie:	Gee I'm sorry about all that. What you need is a friend like Jonathan.
Mo:	Well, he'd better be good at homework! Who is he anyway? I have never heard of a Jonathan around here.
Lizzie:	He's not from around here, Mo. He's in the Bible and he was David's best friend.
Mo:	Was that the kid that knocked Goliath down?
Lizzie:	Yep. The same one.
Mo:	Tell me more Lizzie. I need a Bible story to calm me down.
Lizzie:	Well Jonathan was the king's son and one day he would be king himself. That's the way it works.
Mo:	So, he was "Prince Jonathan".
Lizzie:	Yeah. But David had been told by God that he would be the next king. God was not pleased with King Saul anymore. So King Saul was trying to kill David. He wanted his own son to be king. Trouble was, David and Jonathan were best friends.
Mo:	Oooo! That's getting tricky. These two kids are best friends while the king is trying to kill one of them - David, so the other one, Jonathan will be king.

Lizzie:	I'm proud of you Mo. You got it! But Jonathan knew that God meant for David to be king. And Jonathan really loved David. So, he helped David escape from the king and hide.
Mo:	How did he do that?
Lizzie:	David went out into the paddock outside the palace. Jonathan went to the king to find out if he really was so angry about David that he would try to kill him right then. If it wasn't safe for David, Jonathan would shoot some arrows far away. This would be a sign that David should hide from King Saul.
Mo:	And did it happen like that? Did David have to leave?
Lizzie:	Yeah, it did. But before David went away, he met Jonathan one last time. They were very sad about never seeing each other again. They cried and hugged. They promised to be friends forever.
Mo:	Aw Lizzie, I liked that story. Except maybe the bit about hugging. You sure they hugged each other?
Lizzie:	Well it happened that way Mo. And it shows they were best friends.
Mo:	And I suppose they both believed that God would always watch over them. Gee, I wish Jonathan was my friend today. I could do with a friend like that.
Lizzie:	Mo, you have a friend who is better than Jonathan.
Mo:	Not Jerry!
Lizzie:	Nope! Better than him.

(Turn to audience)

Hey kids! Who's the best friend we can have?

(Jesus)

See Mo, everyone knows Jesus is your best friend!

Ellie and the Pretend Snake

A retelling of Numbers 21

Ellie peered into her baby brother's eyes. He looked fine. His little arms waved about and his sturdy, chubby legs kicked out at her and he giggled. There were still many people outside their tent, talking excitedly about Mizpah and his miraculous escape from death - how he had been bitten by a small black snake and became sicker and sicker. And then the frantic trip across the camp to the pole. Mizpah could hardly stay awake but somehow Father made him look up, up to that silly-looking bronze snake. Even Ellie could have made a better pretend snake from the river clay she sometimes played with. But the pretend snake fixed Mizpah in a second so it must have been okay. Since then the celebrations hadn't stopped.

Ellie swung around and dropped sulkily to her knees - arms crossed, pushing out her bottom lip. "I bet he wasn't even sick in the first place," she shouted to no-one in particular. "I bet there was no snake at all." But she knew that wasn't true. She had seen the snakes herself, and people all over the camp had seen them and were bitten. All of them died too, only Mizpah had got well. And now everyone was making a big fuss of him.

Ellie tried to think of a way all these people might make a fuss of her. She at least would be old enough to appreciate it.

That night Ellie decided she wouldn't eat her evening meal. Perhaps hunger might lead to an illness. And illness might get her some attention from the grown-ups. But her mother didn't even notice when she pushed the bowl away. "Oh yuk - not this again," she complained.

Nobody heard her. "I HATE this stuff!" she shouted louder. "It is disgusting. It tastes like dirt. It's making me SICK!" Ellie jumped up from the table and ran outside. Now her mother came behind her. "Ellie, don't you ever talk like that! God gave us this special food. For thirty years it's just fallen to us from heaven - we should be thankful, instead everyone is grumbling. Ellie didn't want to listen. When her mother tried to gently steer her back inside, she jerked away. "Well maybe God should take notice of everyone and give us some NICE food!" Mother turned and went into the tent, hoping Ellie would follow. But Ellie stayed.

It was night now - pitch black sky except for a fiery glow some distance away over the head of the camp. For as long as Ellie knew they had been moving, following the fire-cloud. Thousands and thousands of people -Father called them their family. They packed up their tents every couple of weeks and walked, no-one seemed to know where, until the people in front stopped. Then the tents were put up again.

Ellie walked around between the sleeping animals. She remembered the day's excitement and Mizpah's illness and she wished again that she could be the centre of attention. Suddenly a movement close by made her look down. There, sliding quickly in and out around the camel's feet was one of those little snakes. It was so small Ellie wondered how it could make anyone sick. Actually, now she thought about it, Mizpah hadn't looked really ill. Not like he had a spotty illness, or a bad cold even. If she let the snake bite her she could run inside and cry loudly about it. She would roll on the floor, moaning and writhing - maybe scratch at her skin.

Ellie bent down and caught the snake easily. It twisted itself around her arm and then - the tiniest prick feeling on her hand. Immediately the snake dropped off her and slithered away.

Nothing. Ellie couldn't feel anything. No pain, nothing.

Nothing, except that fuzziness in her head. It made her feel very sick, and it was good that Father came out to see where she was, for Ellie was beginning to shake all over.

"Now it has happened to our little girl!" Father shouted into the tent, as he scooped her up into his arms. Everyone came then - from everywhere. But Ellie was almost too sick to enjoy the attention she had wanted so badly. "Take her to the pole!" "Do as Moses told us!" People were shouting all around. Ellie heard her mother close to her. She was screaming hysterically. "This happens when she shakes her fist at God!" "Oh no," thought Ellie, "this is because I grumbled about the food - now I might die!"

Very soon she was being carried through the camp to the pole, the same trip they had made earlier for Mizpah. Her father's feet pounding over the sand, sending buckets and baskets flying. Many, many people were following - "Ellie has been bitten," they called as they went, "Our darling Ellie might die," and "How could we go on without her?" The fuzzy feeling in her head was still there, and she wanted to vomit, but Ellie tried to enjoy the fuss. Why, she could hear her name all over the camp.

"Look up. Look up and live," a thousand voices insisted. "You will die if you don't," someone said. Ellie kept her eyes shut tight. "I am not looking at a dumb snake," she thought. "I'll just stay sick for a while longer." Her father was pleading with her, "Open your eyes Ellie, look up. God will make you well. Look at the snake."

"No!" Ellie tried to shout to him, but it just came out as a whisper. "It's a stupid pretend snake and I'm not going to ..." Her throat tightened. The fuzziness in her head turned to pain. It was hard to get a breath. Ellie suddenly got very frightened. It didn't matter that everyone was calling her name, there was only one whose attention she wanted - "God, help me live!" And there she was, looking up at that stupid pretend snake. Ellie felt well again.

Her father carried her home and Mother tucked her into bed. Still there were people bustling outside, wanting to see her and touch her. Ellie told her mother - "Tell them to go away."

God is My Maker

A puppet play for Zoe and Benny

Zoe: Hi Benny, it's been a long time since we've seen you around here, isn't it kids? *(Notices Benny's bandaged arm)* Hey what's wrong with your arm?

Benny: It's a bandage Zoe. I had a little accident yesterday and some of my stuffing started coming out. My mother sewed up the hole but it's still sore.

Zoe: Aw Benny, That's the most ridiculous thing I ever heard!!!

Benny: But it's true Zoe. Here, I'll take the bandage off and show you.

Zoe:	No. No, I don't mean the hole. Puppets get holes in them all the time. I mean that thing you said about a MOTHER. Puppets don't have mothers, only people have mothers. You have a MAKER.
Benny:	You're telling me my mother ISN'T!!
Zoe:	She's just the person who made you. She got all the bits - foam rubber, stretchy fabric, glue, felt and stuffing and sewed you together on a sewing machine.
Benny:	Wow! Hey Zoe, do you have a mother or a maker?
Zoe:	I'm a puppet, same as you. I have a maker too.
Benny:	Same maker as me?
Zoe:	*(thinking)* Hmmm … no I think it's a different one.
Benny:	Zoe, just who makes people? Like all these kids here? Did someone get bits of hair and skin and stuffing and make them?
Zoe:	No silly. They're made inside their mothers. God made people that way so there would be families with Dads and Mums and kids.
Benny:	*(acting smart)* So who made the mothers then?
Zoe:	Well God made everything, Benny. He made the whole world - the mountains and the seas and trees and birds. He made animals and people and stars.
Benny:	Yeah, but where did He get the stuff to make all that out of?
Zoe:	Oh God didn't need to make it out of something. God made everything from nothing.
Benny:	But my maker needed stuffing and glue and foam rubber. What did God use?
Zoe:	He used nothing Benny. Absolutely nothing! That's why He is so great. He is the creator of everything.

Benny:	That means everything belongs to Him, doesn't it? I belong to my maker because she made me.
Zoe:	And I belong to my maker. I'm really glad I was made, Benny.
Benny:	I think the kids out there are glad God made them, aren't you kids?
Zoe:	God made them all different too. See, there's a big kid, and there's one with freckles, and curly hair. Wow! There's not two of them that are the same - not even the twins!!
Benny:	They're nearly the same, Zoe.
Zoe:	And still different, just like us.
Benny:	Gee Zoe, God is the BEST!!!

The Littlest Disciple

A reimagining of Matthew 9:9-11

Simon leaned back against Matthew's legs.

"What's seven multiplied by six?" his uncle asked him.

"7, 14, 21 … times two, forty-two!" he shouted towards the underneath of the table.

"Correct!" Uncle Matthew replied, "though your method is dubious." Most boys would think that sitting on the floor in the tax collector's booth all day would be most tedious and unappealing, but Simon relished it. Not even his uncle enjoyed the job of exacting the taxes out of the citizens anymore. A year ago they'd rise early in the morning and Uncle Matthew would be bristling to start the day at the booth. There was a spring in his step, an excited anticipation of the arguments and mental tricks he would use to get the most money for his bosses. The rows of numbers that once held him in thrall now only caused him to sigh deeply and often. Simon was perplexed by this change.

He heard heavy feet coming to the front of the booth; another merchant ready to do battle with Uncle Matthew. Simon popped up to peer over the table. His uncle pushed him back down, and quietly did his calculations based on the figures the merchant showed him. No arguments, no numerical gymnastics. The merchant was surprised, taken aback. He quickly handed over the coins before the tax collector came to his senses, then turned to hurry away.

"Uncle, are you alright?" Simon asked.

"Hmmmm …" was the only reply he got, so he went back to the game of patterns he had made up. He scored the floor with a stone and counted the numbers of each of the twigs and pebbles, making predictions on what the next number in the sequence should be. When he heard a merchant or Uncle mention a number, he added it to the pattern. Late in the afternoon they closed up the booth and walked home. Uncle Matthew was deep in thought and Simon was still playing number games in his head.

On the following morning something happened that changed everything.

The tax collector and his nephew arrived at the booth as usual; the awning was pulled out, the shutters folded back. Matthew wiped the seat of his bench as he always did, before easing himself on it and opening the ledger.

But then he looked up to see a stranger standing before him.

"You require something, Sir?" He asked.

Simon heard a difference in his uncle's tone. He popped up to take a look at the stranger for himself. Nobody remarkable. Looks like a teacher. Smells like a fisherman.

That thought made Simon duck back behind his uncle.

"Jesus of Nazareth, isn't it?" Matthew said, once he'd taken a closer inspection.

"That's right." The man replied. "And what do I require of you? Nothing less than all of you. Follow me Matthew."

Simon's head appeared again over the edge of the table. This time Uncle didn't push him back down, instead he grabbed the back of his shirt and hauled him all the way out.

"This is my nephew. I'm 'in loco parentis'. Wherever I go he will come too."

"Excellent," said Jesus, and soon Simon and Matthew had the booth shut again and they were following The Teacher.

That was the end of sitting on the floor of the tax collector's booth for Simon. Now he was part of a merry band of men who travelled around with Jesus. At first the other men were astonished to have such a man as Matthew in their company, especially when he decided to throw a party. He wanted Jesus to meet all his friends, except they were mostly tax collectors. The interpreters of the Jewish laws, known as Pharisees, were horrified. Simon had been allowed to attend for awhile; he watched as the guests arrived and he saw the lawyers skulking in the street outside. They weren't invited and they didn't approve of those who had been. Uncle just laughed and filled everyone's tankard with ale.

Simon was the only kid in the travelling group of disciples. Often he spent the days with the women who accompanied them. He helped them at the market or at the laundry, fetching and carrying. One morning he was sitting with one as she calculated the food they needed, and she discovered his gift for understanding numbers. "Well, from now on this can be your job!" she exclaimed.

That evening Jesus found Simon under a sycamore tree. He sat cross-legged beside him. "I've heard that you are good with figures," he said. "We are indeed blessed to have you with us. You must be our littlest disciple." Simon was quiet as he pondered on Jesus' words. *A blessing, yes. But it was he who felt the most blessed.*

For many months Matthew's nephew watched, worked and listened. Matthew took notes on everything that happened and Simon noticed how many *numbers* were in Uncle's account of Jesus' ministry. Fourteen generations from Abraham to David, fourteen from King David to the exile, and another fourteen to Jesus. Fourteen times three, or seven times six … forty-two. Jesus was in the wilderness for forty days and nights. He called twelve disciples (and one little one). He told the crowd that God knew the number of hairs on each head; he fed five thousand and then four thousand. He asked, "can you not buy two birds for a penny?" And talked of walking two miles with the person who asks you to accompany him for one. The littlest disciple embraced each number, turning it over, playing with it, inviting other numbers to join in the fun. Two fish and five loaves multiplied by five thousand. Twelve baskets full of leftovers. Carried by the twelve.

Then one day, as Jesus and his companions entered a small town a different crowd came to meet them. Tired, dusty, and thirsty, the disciples were eager to find the inn where they would be staying. They wanted to have cleaned feet, cool wine, and a comfortable place to recline. Simon trudged behind his uncle and gave voice to the feelings of them all. "I'm so tired Uncle, when will we get there?" In answer Matthew came to a dead stop and let out a low whistle of frustration. "Not any time soon!"

Ahead of them was a collection of women and children, and a few men. Some disciples approached them, listened to their request, then tried to shoo them away. Most of the people stayed where they were. Uncle Matthew and some others began to reason with them: "We are all tired, especially The Teacher. He must rest, and really, these are just little children. The Teacher has more important things to do …"

But Jesus had no more important people to meet than these little ones. He called the disciples to himself and angrily told them to stand aside. They drew back. And as he moved towards the families his littlest disciple ran alongside, slipping his hand into that of his Friend. He watched as Jesus took the children, one by one, into his arms. Placed his hand on their head and blessed them.

Blessed them.

Encountering Jesus

A reflection on Matt 8:28-34

It's a peaceful spot, not too far from town, the ideal place to let the swine wander and graze. Well, most of the time it is. You see, in the tombs up in Gadarenes there are a couple of wild men. People say they are demon possessed.

On this day we saw some other strangers who we now know were Jesus the Nazarite and his disciples. I'd heard of him and I should have recognized him when those two wild men started shouting at him and he ordered their demons to leave them. He's known for that kind of thing.

Well, I have nothing against that man for giving those two their lives back and it's not every day that you witness such a miracle right before your eyes. But it is the other thing that he did that really angered us.

The demons asked him to send them into OUR pigs. Can you believe it?! And then once our herd was filled with demons it ran straight down the bank and into the lake. Every one of the pigs drowned!

Utterly gobsmacked, us herders took off in the other direction – into town, and there we told anyone who'd listen what Jesus had done. A whole posse of townsfolk went back to the "scene of the crime".

Jesus and his followers were still in the field. Once the townies had established what had happened via a whole barrage of questions, they had an impromptu town council meeting. Then they asked Jesus to leave. And I say, "Fair enough! He ruined our livelihood. He ruined our lives."

Lord,

Let me not only see what I may have lost because of my encounter with you. May I continually count the blessings you have bestowed on me. May my following you be about giving back to you, in gratitude, for all I have received.

Amen

Time for Revenge

A puppet play for Mo and Lizzie

Pete – Their human friend

Pete: Mo, Lizzie. How's it going?

Mo: Oh, hi Pete! Lizzie and I have a problem. Could you help us?

Pete: Sure guys. Tell me about it.

Lizzie: It's a girl at school. She's so mean, and she can be a real PAIN. But yesterday she did the meanest thing!

Pete:	Tell me about it guys!
Mo:	Well, there's a little kid who's not real smart. He falls for every trick. Yesterday, Alison told him the principal wanted to see him. Told him he was in big trouble.
Lizzie:	The little kid started to cry and then ...
Mo:	Alison laughed at him. And Lizzie did too!
Lizzie:	*(Making excuses)* Well it was funny to watch him ... I didn't mean to ... But then he dropped his lunch and spilled his drink all down the front ... It WAS funny! Hey, you guys would have done the same.
Mo:	I don't know ...
Lizzie:	Then the principal really did come along. He asked us what happened. Alison pointed to ME, and said, "That girl knocked him over."
Mo:	See what we mean?
Pete:	I think so. But what's the problem you have now?
Lizzie:	I feel bad about laughing at the little kid. But mostly I want to get back at Alison. She got me into trouble. So I want Mo to help me think of a way to pay her back for what she did!
Mo:	I'm not sure we should do that, Pete.
Pete:	It seems like you have two things to do, Lizzie.
Lizzie:	Yeah, What?
Pete:	First you need to ask that little kid to forgive you for laughing at him. And next time help him, don't laugh.
Lizzie:	Hmm ... That could be hard. What's the other thing?

Pete:	Instead of thinking of ways to pay Alison back for being mean, you have to think of ways to show her you love her.
Mo and Lizzie:	Aw! NO WAY!
Pete:	Yep! Jesus tells us to love our enemies - to do good to those who hate you.
Mo:	That's going to be really hard.
Pete:	But if you decide to do it, Jesus will help you.
Lizzie:	How do you figure that, Pete?
Pete:	Because Jesus has promised to help those who trust and obey Him. And don't forget who it was that first forgave you. Even when you laughed, Lizzie.
Mo and Lizzie:	Then let's go ...

Sophia's Pictures

Can you put a child in the midst of Revelation?

Grandfather John has dreams. He tells me they are dream-gifts, given to him by God, while he is in the Spirit.

I'm only nine years old and these are hard things for me to understand. This is why Grandfather John sits on the bench by the white sand and tells me what he saw, and this is why I draw. So, I will understand one day.

"I am the Living One; I was dead, and now look, I am alive for ever and ever! And I hold the keys of death and Hades. Write, therefore, what you have seen, what is now and what will take place later."

"What did this man look like, Grandfather John?"

"He had a white robe with a gold sash. And his hair was also white. Eyes ... yes, eyes of blazing fire! His voice sounded like rushing water ... beautiful, beautiful rushing water."

"I'm not sure I know how to draw sounds, Grandfather."

"Do your best Talitha."

My charcoal stick dances over the paper. I love drawing, it is like air. I need it like I need breath. Soon my old friend is rubbing his scratchy chin. He is done retelling me his dream-gifts for today. "Let's get a cool drink from your mother," he suggests, and I hand him the sheets of paper with my pictures on them.

"These are the words of him who holds the seven stars in his right hand and walks among the seven golden lamp stands."

A week later Grandfather John is standing in the street outside our home. "Are you coming?" he shouts. I turn to my mother. "Yes, yes," she says. "But take some food with you. That man is as thin as a broomstick; he will not have the stamina to tell you of his visions!"

Soon we are on the beach. Grandfather loves to be here. He tells me it reminds him of the time he was a fisherman, and then his times as a disciple of Jesus. I know because I have made pictures of the storm on the lake, and of the miraculous catch.

"How can I draw seven churches?" I ask him.

"I don't know," he replies. "I am the writer of words, not the maker of pictures." He smiles.

I sketch one church on each sheet of paper I have. Seven. Then I hand them to him. He carefully writes the name of each church above it, and hands the sheets back to me. "Ready?" he asks. I hold up my stick of charcoal: "As ever!"

Grandfather John is not really my grandfather. He came to our village when I was a baby, and lives in the house next to ours. Mother tells me he spends all of his time writing, and I know he has written a book. It is called The Good News about Jesus.

The sun is low in the sky when my drawings are finished. Grandfather has eaten all the food. Each piece of paper now has many smaller images inside my outlines of the church. Lamp stands, crowns, a mouth with vomit, a thief, a book of life. Yet every church has the Cross of Jesus on its roof.

"Then I saw another angel flying in midair, and he had the eternal gospel to proclaim to those who live on earth - to every nation, tribe, language and people. He said in a loud voice, "Fear God and give him glory, because the hour of his judgement has come ..."

"More angels, Grandfather?"

"Yes Talitha, a very special one." He tells me.

Grandfather John calls me Talitha. It means little girl in his language. He has also told me about the little girl who Jesus raised from the dead.

Today we sit directly on the sand. Before us there is a small campfire on which Grandfather is cooking sardines, all the while telling me about his newest dream-gift.

"Is it a scary angel? Will it destroy the people?" I ask him.

"All angels are a bit scary my child. Take up your drawing instrument and make me a picture."

He talks and cooks. My charcoal moves gently across the paper until the words that are guiding it change. Now the charcoal needs to be pushed hard to make the darkest black for clouds of doom. Fearful images appear, pointing to a frightening end.

As we eat our cooked lunch I ask Grandfather John if God has told him what is to come. "Yes, and no."

"I saw the Holy City, the new Jerusalem, coming down out of heaven from God, prepared as a bride beautifully dressed for her husband."

Mother has once again given me a parcel of food for Grandfather John. There will be no walk down to the white sand because, she tells me, he is in his little house, sick in his bed. But when I go in he is tying his sandals on and invites me into the courtyard. He looks tired but not sick.

"Did you bring your drawing materials?"

"I have," I answer.

"There are things that God has shown to me, Talitha, and he says I must write it down. Your pictures help me remember."

"Have you found out how it ends? I want to draw something happy."

In the cool shade under the vines Grandfather begins to talk. And my charcoal stick is once again skipping over the paper. A throne for a lamb, a holy city with jewels on its gates, a beautiful bride, a river of life, and trees that grow fruit all year. The servants of God with His Name on their foreheads.

I look at Grandfather John, at his forehead. I make a quick sketch of him on my page and write 'God' across the top of his face.

"Hallelujah! For our Lord God Almighty reigns. Let us rejoice and be glad and give him glory!"

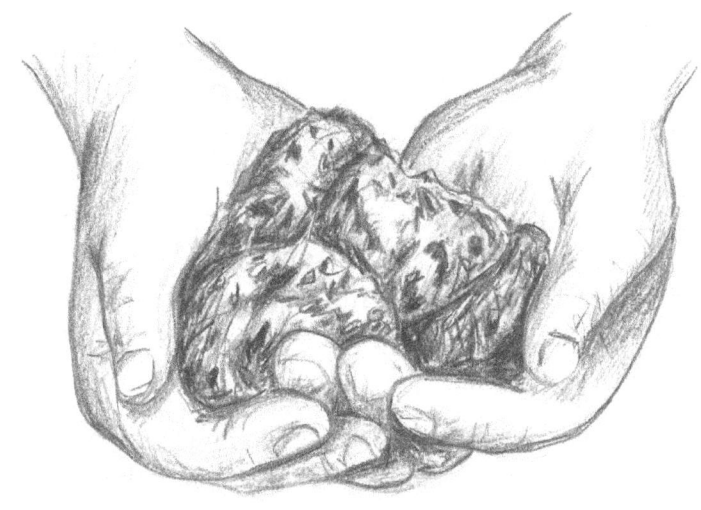

Feeding of the 5000

A reflection on Mark 6:30-44.

It's been a busy morning. We started with a debriefing, telling Jesus what's been going on. The teaching, the healing, the people. Oh, the people! They just keep coming! I was relieved when Jesus suggested going over the lake to a quiet field and just relaxing for a spell. But from the water we could see the crowds following us along the shoreline. My heart sank; couldn't we have a moment to ourselves?

As we stepped onto the shore the people caught up with us. Jesus kept walking as if he could shake them off, or perhaps hoping they would realise we wanted some time away from them. I know that's what the rest of us were hoping.

No, he wasn't walking from them. He was leading them. He wasn't trying to shake them off. He was gathering them closer. When we reached the quiet green-grassy hill where we should have had our restful afternoon, Jesus directed the crowd to sit.

Then he taught them. Not the "rules and regulations" kind of teaching you can usually get from the rabbis, but stories. Stories about ordinary folk – shepherds, widows, arguing brothers and the like. My favourite was the good shepherd one. Imagine leaving 99 sheep and going off after one stupid lamb! I guess it's like that Psalm King David wrote – the good shepherd will always care for his sheep, even the stupid little ones.

Well, I reckon it's time to send this lot home. It's getting on to dinner time and if they're like us they won't have had lunch either. Jesus is talking to Peter. I can't believe it! He wants us to feed everyone!

James is scouting around in case someone's brought enough food for 5000 people. Well, that's not going to happen. He comes back with a meagre 5 loaves and 2 fish (and the kid whose dinner it was), and hands them to Jesus. As if it were a banquet spread out for a king, Jesus holds them up to the sky and thanks God for the bounty.

I'm calculating that every man, woman and child might get a crumb each and they'll probably start a riot to get that much.

Jesus gives me a handful of bread – no, it's more than an armful. I walk among the people who calmly take what they need. Some take a bit more, and when I get back to Jesus he again fills my arms with provisions. The people have eaten all they want. Now they are lounging in the grass patting their bellies with satisfaction. "No thanks, mate," they say. We collect the leftovers and bring it back to Jesus.

Jesus, like a shepherd, lead us.
Much we need thy tender care.
In thy pleasant pastures feed us.
All our sins and grief to bear.

Today I was a stupid little lamb. I started well – focused on Jesus, following him, listening to him. But I wandered.

I focused on myself – my need for rest, my hunger, me, me, me.

I stopped listening even when He was speaking loudly with His actions.

I was hungry even when I had my arms full of food.

Lord, forgive me my blind stupidity.

Hook your shepherd's staff around my neck and bring me close to you again.

Because that's where I want to be.

Amen

God Takes The Shakes Away

A puppet play for Mo and Zoe

Based on Acts 20:22 -24

Mo: Hi Zoe. I've got a quiz question for you.

Zoe: Mo. How did you know I like doing quizzes?

Mo: Just a wild guess. You ready?

Zoe: Yep, fire away.

Mo: What's the all-time scariest thing you can think of?

Zoe:	Is this a trick question?
Mo:	No … o … o…! Come on! I want the very, hairiest-scariest situation you could ever find yourself in.
Zoe:	Well … Let me see … *(in story-telling voice)* Me and Mel Gibson are crawling through the darkest underground tunnel, on our stomachs, towards a secret inner chamber, where the mummified body of Tooten-kar-man lies in a golden casket. When SUDDENLY …
Mo:	*(listening intensely)* Yeah???
Zoe:	A THOUSAND RATTLESNAKES FALL ON THE GROUND IN FRONT OF US!!!

Mo screams and Zoe, having scared herself, screams too.

Zoe:	*(regains composure)* Okay. Okay. What's with the silly questions anyway?
Mo:	Oh, we were just learning about courage in Sunday School.
Zoe:	Sorry Mo, but it doesn't take courage to go to Sunday School. Unless you're in David's class.
Mo:	No Zoe! We were talking about how Paul was very courageous.
Zoe:	Paul was that guy who kept getting himself thrown into prison, and shipwrecked, wasn't he?
Mo:	Yeah, and all because he couldn't keep his big mouth shut.
Zoe:	He talked too much??
Mo:	He talked plenty, and always about the same thing - well, the same person - Jesus. He couldn't stop telling everyone that they should believe in God and in Jesus being their Saviour.

Zoe:	Didn't the people want him to say that?
Mo:	Some people didn't. Some people didn't want him to talk because it stirred things up. Then they threatened to kill him.
Zoe:	Wow Mo … I bet he was shaking in his boots. That must have been his "HAIRIEST, SCARIEST" situation!!!
Mo:	Nah! I don't think so, Zoe. Paul relied on God. God gave him strength to keep on talking. God gave him courage.
Zoe:	Maybe God really needed Paul to spread the Good News about Jesus. So He took the shivers and the shakes right out of him.
Mo:	*(thinks for a moment)* Sometimes God does that to me too, Zoe.
Zoe:	Really?
Mo:	When I want to do something but it's too scary - like tell my friends about Jesus. First, I'm really nervous. I'm scared of what they'll think of me or do to me. Then God takes the shakes away and I can say what I want to.
Zoe:	With great courage!!
Mo:	And Thanks to God!!!!

"Samuel - Answer to my prayer"

A retelling of Samuel 1-3

Peeking out from behind the column, Samuel saw the most wonderful thing. Four little children came running across the courtyard, skipping happily in the early morning sunlight towards the portico where Samuel stood. They were his brothers and sisters. But the best thing for Samuel was seeing the woman who followed them. This year she looked especially beautiful. This year she was expecting a baby.

With a squeal of joy, he came out from his hiding place. He quickly bounded down the steps. "Samuel! Samuel!" his brothers and sisters shouted, arms outstretched towards him. But Samuel ran right past them, only slowing to exchange a few high-fives with his brothers. He kept running till he reached his mother. They hugged for a long time, then stepping back he stared carefully at her.

"Mama, you're so …"

"Big, I think the word is. I am really too big with this baby to be travelling, but I had to come."

"No Mama, I meant that you are so beautiful." Samuel said.

"You are a good son 'Samuel, answer to my prayer'. Now go and play."

This was his once-a-year chance to be a boy. A boy with brothers to wrestle with and sisters to tease. Asaph and Gershon kicked a round ball between them while Samuel tried to catch it with his feet. They were good and he was out of practice.

Finally he tackled Gershon to the ground, and the three were tumbling over and over.

"Samuel, come and talk to us." His sisters called from the steps. Samuel left his brothers with the ball and went over to Miriam and Judith. They were pretty like their mother. They moved apart to make room for him in between. As he sat down Miriam pushed her fingers into his ribs. "Ouch!" he cried. But then Judith was tickling him mercilessly. "Oh stop it. I thought you wanted to talk." "Oh yeah," Miriam said, and they did stop. "Do you want to hear our little song?" Samuel nodded, "Sure."

The sun was setting as Samuel and his family sat around the big table eating their meal. They chattered about this and that. His father tall and wise, his mother's round smiling face bringing joy to them all. And all the children - how he loved them.

Afterwards Samuel and his mother went to his room. They always did this, every year the same. He sat at her feet with his head in her lap. "Mama, tell me again about my name – 'Samuel, answer to my prayer'." His hand moved across her huge stomach. It wasn't smooth. There were lumps and bumps - moving lumps and bumps. His mother's words were familiar; he knew the story well. Hannah had prayed for a child, over and over again. And when he, Samuel had been born, she promised to give him back to God. Now he lived in the Temple with Eli the old priest and only saw his family once a year at Passover.

Suddenly a thought struck him. "Was I inside you Mama, like this baby?" "Yes, you were Samuel." The baby pushed against his hand. "Did I move around and bump you like this little baby is doing?" "You did. And every time I praised God in Heaven." "And when I was born you told God He could have me back?"

"You were Samuel. God's answer to my prayers."

Samuel and his mother sat quietly for a time. Then he asked- "Did you pray for me a lot Mama?"

"Oh yes. A thousand prayers and buckets full of sad tears too. I wanted a child very much."

Samuel thought a while. "Mama, I want to know how to pray to God like that. Like He and I are friends, and He would listen to my heart and answer."

"One day Samuel it will be so." His mother said.

And one day it was so ...

Samuel had worked hard today. It was nearly Sabbath and the Temple needed to be cleaned. He had polished the furniture till he could see himself grinning back in the shiny woodwork. He swept the floors, moving across the huge courtyard by marking off the cracks in the paving. Now he lay on his bed and listened to the sounds of the night. Close by was the Ark of the Covenant. Close but still behind a heavy curtain. Nearer was the Lamp, burning brightly. Samuel closed his eyes and tried to imagine all those things around him that he had never seen. What did the Ark really look like? What else was behind that curtain? In his heart Samuel knew one day he would see it, one day he would be like Eli, a servant of God, a priest. Suddenly Samuel jumped up.

What was Eli doing calling him in the middle of the night? Quickly he tumbled out of bed and scuttled across the court to Eli. "Here I am Eli," he said, rubbing the sleep from his eyes.

"I didn't call you," said the old man, "better go back to bed young man." Samuel ran back across the court with icy feet slipping on the cold paving. Into bed he crawled, shivering as he tucked the rugs around himself. Soon he was dozing. Just as he felt himself fall into a deep sleep, he heard the voice again ..." *"Samuel"*

Was Eli playing a game with him? Once again Samuel got out of his warm bed and hurried across the court. Perhaps Eli had remembered why he wanted him. "Here I am Eli," he said.

"I didn't call", Eli replied, already his eyelids were drooping shut.

Samuel turned and went back. Now he was very awake. He lay in the flickering light of the lamp for a long time. He knew the voice would come again. And it did. *"Samuel."*

He started to wonder if it really was Eli. The voice sounded close to him. But he couldn't think who else it could be, so he rose out of bed and went back to Eli. The old man hadn't been sleeping either. He looked at Samuel with his eyes as big as plates. "Next time," he told Samuel, "when the Lord calls, you are to answer Him, 'Please speak to me Lord, your servant is listening.'"

Samuel opened and closed his mouth several times, but he didn't know what to say. Lots of thoughts were in his head. It was God who had called him! It was God's voice he had heard. Many times his mother had told him about her prayers to God, and he knew he had been God's answer. Now Samuel was going to answer God himself.

This time across the court he hardly noticed the cold paving and when he reached his bed Samuel leapt into it with joy. "God's going to talk to me!" The thought shouted itself over and over. "Shh!" he told himself, and he lay as still and straight as he could. And he waited.

Samuel sensed someone close by like before. "Are you there?" he whispered. Then it happened.

"Samuel, Samuel!" Words that sounded warm and safe. A voice that made him think of his mother.

"Speak Lord, your little servant is listening." And Samuel did feel very little. And God didn't seem just big. He seemed to fill every part of the Temple – behind the curtain, in the lamplight, even under Samuel's bed. But His words were as near as a friend's whisper.

God told Samuel things he could barely understand. They were frightening and scary things about what God would do in their country and about Eli and his family. And Samuel lay still until morning, never sleeping for a moment. He knew that God didn't see him as a little boy anymore. Now he was someone God wanted to talk with. He knew a great adventure was about to start.

In the morning Samuel jumped out of bed and ran to the Temple doors. He opened them up and looked out at the country. He felt Eli's arm on his shoulder. "What did He say, Samuel?" He had to answer. He had to tell. From now on, whatever God says to him he will have to tell others. That will be his task for all his life.

Five children run through the streets towards the Temple. The littlest is a long way behind, his chubby legs unable to keep up. His mother scoops him up and begins to run. Samuel is running too, past his brothers and sisters to his mother. She stops and puts the toddler down. Samuel grabs both her hands, dancing her round and round.

"He spoke to me Mama. He spoke to me."

Quietly his mother murmurs, "Answer to my prayer."

Saul on the road to Damascus

By Jacqui Stok

This is Saul
Saul is Paul
This is Saul and Saul is Paul

This is Amman
Amman loves God's Son
Amman loves God's Son and God's Son loves Amman.

Saul hates Amman cos Amman loves God's Son
Saul hurts Amman cos Amman loves God's Son
He kicks Amman's shin
Pokes Amman with a pin
He plays dirty tricks
He gives Amman kicks
He locks Amman's head

And puts snakes in his bed.

Saul's mean to Amman

Cos Amman loves God's Son

Saul has a plan

Saul has a plan to jail that man

That man called Amman

Cos Amman loves God's Son

Saul makes his way

To Damascus one day

To see to the plan

That would jail that man

That man called Amman

Cos Amman loves God's Son.

Suddenly there came a light

That light was bright

Gave Saul a fright

He lost his sight

It was as dark as night

There came a voice from the sky
That asked Saul why
He was mean to Amman
Cos Amman loves God's Son

This part is the best
For you never will guess
Whose voice that was
But I'll tell you because
It was Jesus God's Son
The very same one
Who is loved by Amman
Saul had better start to run

Then Jesus told Saul
Who was also called Paul
To make his way
To Damascus that day

And wait for a man
That would tell Saul God's plan

Saul did as Jesus said
But he had to be led
Cos he'd lost his sight
From that light that was bright

Ananias was a man
Who was part of God's plan
While he was eating some bread
God put a vision in his head
Ananias was told
that he had to be bold
And go visit Saul
Who was also called Paul
And restore his sight
That was lost from that light

Ananias was sad

He knew Saul was bad
And that Saul hurt Amman
Cos Amman loved God's Son
Ananias was blue
He loved Jesus too

But God had a plan
Saul was God's man
He'd preach the good news
And suffer the blues

So Ananias went to Saul
Who was also called Paul
And he gave Saul back his sight
That was lost from that light
Saul was baptized that very day
His sins were washed away
And he called on Jesus' name
And the Holy Spirit came
Saul's life would never be the same.

Now before we leave today

We have one more thing to say

Jesus died for each of you

And he loves you dearly too

Even if you're mean or if you're mad

Or you've done something really bad

He has a special plan

For every girl, boy, woman and man

So call on Jesus' name

And you'll never be the same.

Hiding

A story based on Luke 2:41-52

Can you think of the best place for a boy to hide?

Well, I know lots of good spots, and so does Yeshu, but I looked in most of them and so did his parents. And we still couldn't find him.

My name is Manaen. Everyone calls me Manny, and Yeshu is my good friend. That night I knew he was hiding before anybody else did. I'd worked out he was missing since early that morning.

We are always together, him and me. At school we sit side by side, we play ball in the street outside his house every afternoon, and right after his Pa shows him something new to do in the carpenter's shop, Yeshu shows me. He is a good teacher. Our favourite thing to do, when the chores are done, is to go into the hills to play among the rocks and bushes. There are excellent places to hide up there. Once I spent ages looking for him and you'll never guess where Yeshu was. Right in the middle of some briars! He was sitting there with a stray sheep in his arms.

So you see, when Joseph and Mary called to me and asked me if I knew where their son was, I thought, sure, he could be anywhere. But I just shrugged and said, "Yeshu is good at hide and seek!" His mother wailed. His father frowned. My father took a hold of my ear and marched me away.

A week ago a whole lot of us from Nazareth left to go to Jerusalem for the Passover feast. All the oldest boys at our school were excited, especially because we were allowed to travel together; it was like a big, moving, party. The grownups walked and talked while us youngsters raced ahead. We played games, collected flowers, caught little skinks among the rocks, and chased one another. Yeshu was with us all that time, I'm sure of it.

Then we arrived in the city and, at first, our parents kept us close to them and our freedom was over. Each family stayed in a different place and I didn't see much of my friend until the evening. All the people from Nazareth ate the evening meal together; it was so much fun. Because afterwards we slipped into the streets and continued with our games of hide and seek. Yeshu is as quick as a skink, darting along between the legs and robes of the crowds, ducking behind barrels or making himself invisible in a darkened doorway.

When he actually disappeared - I mean when his parents couldn't find him on the way back home - I just thought, 'Yeshu is so good at hiding he could be in any of a dozen places'. And that's what I told them.

Everyone went quiet as soon as Yeshua's father and mother began the dash back towards Jerusalem. All the grownups were worried. Our group of schoolboys followed our parents to their lodgings without the usual complaints or begging for some more time to goof around in the streets. I went to bed and fell asleep right away. The next morning Yeshu was back amongst the caravan of travellers.

Nobody had to wonder where he had been hiding, Joseph and Mary were telling the whole group. They'd found him in the Temple. What a perfect hideout! I couldn't wait to get him alone and ask what stroke of genius led him to conceal himself there!

Well, when I did catch up to him he was in a good mood and ready to tell me about it. Not the hiding place though, because he hadn't really been trying to hide at all. We spent the remainder of the trip home talking about his father, which is what he and the temple priests had been discussing yesterday. It muddled my brain. Yeshu's father is a carpenter in our town. What do the priests want to know about him? "Manny" my friend told me, "I am the Son of the one true God. The Temple is the house of my Father and I needed to be there."

I have to think on that for a bit.

I've heard about Jesus ...

A reflection on Matt 8:5-13

I've heard about Jesus; water, evil spirits, diseases, they all obey his word. So when he said he would come and heal my servant, I told him plainly, "That's not necessary. Just say the word and I know he will be cured." I knew he would have made the journey for me and the young man, but he is the 'Chief Officer' and what he says goes. But I wasn't expecting his amazement at my reply. And those comments about my faith – surely, I'm not as good as all those pious Jews?!

Jesus comes for each of us. He makes no distinction between masters and servants, Jews or Gentiles. He only requires our faith in him.

Remind me that you are

the Way,

the Truth

and the Life

and apart from you there is no life.

Amen

The Conscript

A story based on Acts 6:8 to the end of chapter 7

"Get up! Get up!"

Issy opened his eyes and jumped from his bed in one swift movement. What was happening? Why were people yelling at him? Where were his parents? Rough hands pulled him outside where he stood blinking in the bright morning light. And then he saw his uncles and his father. "What?" He started to say.

"You're coming with us today." His uncle snarled, while tugging Issy along with the group. "You're a man now, but if you aren't yet, this will make a man of you!"

Issy didn't think of himself as a man. He was ten years old and until now his main tasks were to attend school and to help his mother and grandmother. He carried their shopping when they went to the market every week. He cleaned the animals' pen and put clean straw in the byre. He thought this was what ten-year-olds were expected to do, not to become a man overnight.

He found it hard to keep up with the men. Where were they going? Why were they so angry?

The temple courts were full of angry people. Issy slipped his hand into that of his father's as the crowd pressed forward. Whatever event they were here for was taking place behind closed doors. Yet the crowd wanted answers. "What are they saying?" the men demanded to know about the Sanhedrin priests and lawyers. "What is that blasphemer saying?" they wanted to know about the young man standing before those priests and lawyers.

The information they sought came in hot shards of incendiary words; words that threatened to set off an explosion of such violence that nothing could quench it. Issy squeezed his eyes shut and squeezed his father's hand. Suddenly his father released his grip and glared at his son. "No more," he growled. "Today you will be a man."

Oh, the fear Issy felt as he was carried along on the tide of righteous rage! His feet pounded on the road out of the city but it was as if the people around him had his body in their grip, and he was propelled forward by their very will. Where was his father all this time? Issy didn't know. The crowd was funnelled along the narrow street and through the city gate. On and on the angry mob moved, taking a frightened ten-year-old boy with it.

At last they came to a halt on a hill overlooking a dip in the landscape. In the centre of the hollow stood a young man surrounded by several priests. The questions they asked and the answers he gave were barely audible to the simmering crowd. But when the priests raised their arms to call damnation to come from heaven, the people reached a boiling rage in moments. Issy could not take his eyes off the young man. There was nothing remarkable about him and yet he had strength, a stature, a serenity, that defied the perilous place he was in.

Issy too was in a perilous place. Someone took his hand and shoved a rock into it. "Be the first," he heard the man say. It was his uncle. "I can't", replied Issy, letting the rock fall. It was swiftly replaced. "I order you to throw!" His uncle shouted. The child threw.

Hours later he stumbled into his mother's kitchen. His arms ached from the many times he'd been forced to pick up a stone and hurl it at the young man in the hollow. His eyes stung, his face streaked with the tears that had ceaselessly run down his cheeks. His chest hurt as he'd tried to gulp down the fear and shame and guilt.

Issy was still a child.

Lord,

Guide the thoughts of those grownups who read this, that they may find you in the story, and strive to make your world a better place for the children such as Issy. To your glory.

Amen

Jesus Clears the Temple

A reflection on: John 2:13-16

I'm right behind Jesus. Since he did that miracle with the wine at the wedding, I want to see everything he does. This seemed like a routine visit to the temple … until …

I'm on my way home. I have to give some serious thought to what I've just seen. Jesus was a man out of control, or was he? What did he mean when he said, "My father's house"? That would make him … the son of God! Can that be true? What about the line about destroying the temple? If, if, someone destroyed such a structure it would take more than three days to build it again. It would take another miracle.

I'm sticking with this guy. Whatever he does next, I'm going to be there to see it.

Lord,

Help me to keep my eyes on you. Not because I have to witness the miraculous, wonderful as that would be, but because you are the one who made me. You love me more than anyone else would. Stepping with you will be the best way I could travel through life. You know what will cause me to stumble, and if I'm close to you, you'll gently take my arm and tell me, "Watch that stone there, Hetty. Don't trip over." Thank you Jesus for being the best travelling partner.

Amen

Honesty

A puppet play for Zoe and Benny

Zoe: I wonder where Benny is? He said he would meet me here. Benny's been to KIDS PRAISE and he said he would tell me all about it. I wish he would hurry up!

(Benny Enters)

Benny: Oh boy, oh boy, Zoe, am I excited! You should have been there. It was so great! I learned to play a didgeridoo, and I sang up on the stage, and I ...

Zoe: Hold it a minute Benny. Slow down. *(pause)* I see you've got a new hat.

Benny:	Yeah. Cool, hey?!! It was a prize for playing the didgeridoo the best. I was the champ!
Zoe:	Really? I didn't think they gave out prizes.
Benny,	Well they did ... Just this once ... Just to me... *(slower and quieter)* Because I was the best ... at the didgeridoo ...
Zoe:	Benny, is this true?
Benny:	Yeah. Honestly.
Zoe:	*(doesn't believe him)* Benny. Tell me where you got the hat! Really!
Benny:	I really got it for a prize. Just me.
Zoe:	It's not the truth. I can see it on your face.
Benny:	Aw, Zoe! You sound like my Mum!
Zoe:	Just tell me where you got the hat!!
Benny:	Oh alright then. But you have to promise not to dob on me.
Zoe:	Just tell me.
Benny:	Yeah, well, see I was walking along and there it was on the ground. There was no-one around. I couldn't see anyone who might have dropped it. So I picked it up and put it on.
Zoe:	You didn't hand it in to Lost Property??
Benny:	It's such a cool hat, Zoe. I wanted it. I wanted to keep it.
Zoe:	Benny, why did you tell me you won it?
Benny:	Well, it's better than saying I STOLE IT. I was afraid you would dob me in.

Zoe:	And I still might Benny. But you're not the only person to have told a lie because you were scared to tell the truth. Even Jesus' disciple, Peter, did it.
Benny:	You're kidding me. A good man like Peter the disciple told a lie?
Zoe:	He told three lies. Three times people asked him if he knew Jesus and three times he said no.
Benny:	What was he scared of?
Zoe:	He thought they would call the soldiers and arrest him. Jesus had already been arrested and Peter was afraid they would get him too.
Benny:	So he told them he didn't know Jesus at all …? Wow!!
Zoe:	Peter was a good man who really loved Jesus. He was just really scared.
Benny:	*(sorrowfully)* At least he didn't steal anything from a little kid!
Zoe:	You know Benny, we can fix that. Let's post this hat back to KIDS PRAISE, and they might find its owner.
Benny:	Yeah. What a great idea. And I've got some money in my piggy-bank to buy my own.
Zoe:	That's the way, Benny. You're a champ!

A Child in their Midst

A retelling of Matthew 18, Mark 9 and Luke 9

Let me tell you a story that was once told to me. It's a great tale, but just one among many, so the tellers didn't embellish their stories with finer details. However, I will, and along the way I'll reimagine some colours and shades. I believe this is permissible as long as the listeners are open to God's message in the story.

The Rabbi's disciples were walking towards Capernaum with their Messiah. The road was dusty, the sun was hot, and their tempers were fraying. Jesus walked a little way ahead of them and their argument.

Soon they arrived at the house of some friends and were eagerly welcomed and ushered through the house to the shady courtyard beyond. A servant girl came with tall beakers full of cold wine.

Slowly the heat drained from the faces of the guests as they relaxed after the long walk.

"So," Jesus asked them, "what were you arguing about on the road?"

Before they could answer a ball skittered across the courtyard, rolled under the table and between the legs of the disciples, and was followed by a bevy of little boys. Mayhem ensued while the ball, the legs, and the children battled together. And then peace again, as the boys skipped back to the lane with their prize.

"The argument?" Jesus reminded his disciples.

But no one wanted to say. They squirmed in their seats, they blushed. Finally one of them spoke. "We were discussing who of us is the greatest." It sounded so lame now, when it was spoken out loud to the Rabbi. Not an hour ago they had been in hot contention, firing Scripture missiles at each other, cutting one another down to size, tearing at each other's egos. It had been as if their place in Eternity mattered on who was crowned greatest of all.

Jesus let the disciples' words hang in the air for a moment. Then he called out to one of the boys.

"Here, come here son." The lad came over.

Jesus beckoned to the servant girl. "Please bring the boy a drink."

She went away and returned with a beaker of lemonade. She handed it to the boy who took it in his dusty hands. Then she gave him a straw. Immediately he began slurping noisily.

"I tell you, unless you become like a little child, you will not enter the Kingdom of Heaven. Unless you lower yourself to the position of the least, you will have no position in Eternity."

"Really?" The disciples thought. "Were their ears deceiving them? What could Jesus be saying?"

But Jesus hadn't finished the lesson.

"Whoever welcomes one of these little ones, welcomes me. But whoever rejects them, it would be better if that man were thrown into the sea with a lump of Rome's finest concrete around his neck!"

The boy looked up from his now-empty beaker. He smiled at Jesus as if they shared the best secret. He wiped the back of his hand across his mouth. And then he belched.

Melchior, Balthazar, and Caspar

A retelling of Matthew 2: 1-12

It was a black night. Nothing lit our Eastern sky, nothing. The tiny pinpricks of starry light were almost blotted out by the inky darkness.

Nevertheless, our team was out there on the dunes, peering into our telescopes, occasionally lighting a small candle to jot notes and diagrams onto our parchments.

It was a still night, which was a good thing. Sand grit can be a problem if it's blown into our equipment and ink. Caspar was sitting in the middle of a huge groundsheet, gazing across to the horizon. It was so quiet that, even though I had my back to him, I heard it when he stopped breathing. He wasn't dead, just dead surprised.

I turned and said, "Cas?" and then looked where I thought he was looking.

I answered his unspoken question. "I think it is."

"I'm going to make a light" he said, "you get Melchior."

I set out over the dunes. With no illumination I stumbled along. Once I turned to look behind me and saw Caspar's small candle. But behind him was a rising glow from near the horizon. I finally found Mel; actually, I stumbled onto him. He cursed as I landed on him, causing his 'scope to drop to the ground.

"Look" I said, and standing close behind him with my arm alongside his head, I pointed to the west. He moved slightly to follow my direction. "Yes …" he murmured.

"Are you thinking what I'm thinking?" I asked.

"I think I am, Balthazar!" he replied, and I heard the twinkle in his eyes.

We ran then, back to Caspar, who had been consulting the charts. He was fairly jumping out of his skin. And that's not bad for an eighty-year-old astronomer.

This was the beginning of our journey westward. That little star, rising up into our world, had been predicted for centuries. But not as headline news in the 'Astronomers Of The East' Gazette. No. It was hidden in the historical parchments of our discipline, to be discovered through intense cross referencing and study. A group of us were hoping and waiting for its appearance in our lifetime. And here it was!

The following days were a buzz of preparations and talking. Our colleagues agreed that Mel, Caspar and I should be the ones to meet the promised King. The King born somewhere to the west of us. The King whose star we had seen rising in the darkness.

And this King would be worshipped with gifts.

So a committee was formed to find appropriate gifts. The gift registrars. They consulted the astronomical charts too, for clues. Each gift would be fraught with meaning. Finally, they came on the night before we were to set out. Three packages were presented to us.

"This one is the only gift we could give to a new King," one said. "It is the ultimate symbol of power and majesty." Caspar stood beside me and whispered breathlessly, "Gold!"

"This one," another registrar said, holding up a small box, "was a tricky one. Something in our research suggested this new King is also Godly. So in this box is the very precious frankincense." He handed it to Melchior.

A third registrar stepped forward.

"Finally, our last gift." A few of the other members of the committee shuffled uneasily and looked down, as if they weren't too sure about this choice of a gift.

"Myrrh." And it was offered to me.

An explanation was called for. The registrar continued. "It's traditionally used as an embalming agent. The committee thought it appropriate as all kings eventually die, and this new King will deserve the very best of burials. Although," he added, "this King is a God, so it should not be necessary. However, on the off chance …" He was now clearly out of his depth so I stepped forward and took the package from him. He looked glad to be rid of it.

The journey continued. The next morning we were assisted onto our camels and the whole assembly of astronomers were there to see us off. Our College President handed us the scrolls containing copies of the prophesies of the Hebrew, Daniel, concerning the King we were seeking. And so, we left our home in the East.

It was together boring and exhilarating to be travelling.

At night we pitched our tent, found our telescopes and studied the sky as we had always done. But we hardly needed the telescope to see that Star; it became larger and brighter every night. It was our signpost, our route map, our light for our path. During the days I re-read Daniel's prophesy. He was an alien in our country, captured over 500 years ago and brought to Babylon as booty. He wrote about his God and a plan to bring a saving Christ into the world. The 'Son of Man coming from Heaven'.

When we reached the region of Palestine we made our way straight to the city of Jerusalem. I was glad to stop there. Beyond this country was the Mare Nostrum sea and I didn't like sailing much. I preferred the ships of the desert - camels, and the waves of bare sand.

At the palace the guards brought us before the ruler, King Herod. He listened to the reason for our coming, and looked puzzled. "No new kings here!" he blustered.

"A newborn King, a baby perhaps?" I suggested.

Now he looked positively scary. "No newborns around here!!" Melchior offered another idea, "We believe him to be the king of the Jews."

"What?!!" roared Herod. "I am the king of the Jews!"

And then, "Send for my advisors, and those magicians I have!"

They came, and they confirmed what we had said. In the town of Bethlehem the Christ would be born.

Now Herod ordered us out of the room while he conferred with his advisors.

We sat in a tiny anteroom, cooling our heels. "I don't like that man much," said Caspar, "can't we just go over to that town and check it out for ourselves?"

But then the door opened and we were called back in.

Herod's plan went like this:

We were to go to Bethlehem, find the baby King, and then return to Herod and give him the precise location.

It was something about the way his moustache twitched when he spoke that made me wonder. His whole demeanour had changed since before, but that moustache was twitching! I didn't trust him.

Well, we found Bethlehem, and we found the King. Our star continued to lead us until it stopped over an ordinary-looking house in a plain old street. No palace, no royal crib, no red carpet.

We felt a tiny bit overdressed for the occasion, and the gifts we brought seemed a tad too grand for such an ordinary child, but we knelt before him. His parents didn't blink. It was as if they knew His importance, as if they understood *Who* he really was.

I bowed deeply.

I offered the jar of myrrh to the child's mother.

In my heart I felt some flutter of recognition as I gazed upon the small boy sitting on his mother's knee.

The star had brought me to Him. He was the end of my journey.

Mud – The Story of Jeremiah

A puppet play for Mo and Lizzie

Mo: *(singing)* Jeremiah was a Bullfrog, da, da, da…

Lizzie: Mo! Jeremiah was not a bullfrog!

Mo: Yes he was! He was wet, and slimy, and sitting in a puddle of MUD. That sounds like a bullfrog to me.

Lizzie: Jeremiah was in the Bible, Mo. He was a prophet of God. I don't know where you got your story of a bullfrog from, but it wasn't in the Bible.

Mo:	Well, that's where you're wrong, smarty pants, Bizzy Lizzie! You just sit back and let **me** tell **you** this Bible story.
Lizzie:	Go ahead Mo.
Mo:	Well Jeremiah wasn't really a bullfrog …
Lizzie:	Told you so!
Mo:	… but he was stuck in the mud. And you were right about him being a prophet of God. He told the King of Judah that if the country didn't turn back to God, then some other country would come and capture them all. They would be dragged off and treated like slaves. And that would be the end of Judah. Gone forever!
Lizzie:	*(impatiently)* I'm waiting for the mud, Mo.
Mo:	Yeah, I'm coming to that. So, the King didn't listen. Jeremiah went all through the city streets yelling out about the end of Judah and slaves and stuff like that. All the people said, "Get this bad-news-guy out of here!" Soon everyone was sick of Jeremiah. They complained to the King. He said, "Okay, do what you want to shut him up."
Lizzie:	I know what they did! They filled his mouth up with MUD!
Mo:	NO LIZZIE! They chucked him into a well. There was no water, just lots of mud. In the well, Lizzie. It was slimy, and oozzy, and DISGUSTING!
Lizzie:	Serves him right for telling all that bad news.
Mo:	Well he wasn't there for long. Someone came and pulled him out.

	And he went right back to the King and told him to listen to God.
Lizzie:	Did the King listen?
Mo:	Nope. No-one listened.
	And everything happened like God said. The whole country was destroyed and the people taken away.
Lizzie:	*(sad)* That Jeremiah was nothing but a bad-news-guy! I think I'd like him better if he was a BULLFROG.
Mo:	There was some good news, Lizzie.
	Jeremiah told the people that God would stay with them wherever they were. Then one day He would show them the way back home. To Jerusalem.
Lizzie:	Gee Mo, God really loves His people even when they're bad.
Mo:	Like He really loves us, even when we're bad.
Lizzie:	That reminds me of Jesus. God gave us Jesus because He loves us. He gave us a second chance, like those people with Jeremiah.
Mo:	You're getting smarter, Lizzie!

Noodle in a Haystack

Noodle was a little mouse.

He lived with all of his family right in the middle of a big haystack.

One day Noodle, together with his brothers, sisters, and cousins, sat with his Auntie Needle while she told stories and knitted.

Suddenly Noodle asked her, "Auntie Needle, WHERE IS GOD?" Auntie stopped knitting and pointed up.

"Up there." She said.

So the next day Noodle started to climb. Up the inside of the haystack. One bale at a time.

When he got to the top he saw bright blue everywhere. It was very big. He blinked his eyes. It was bigger than two little pink mouse-eyes could look at.

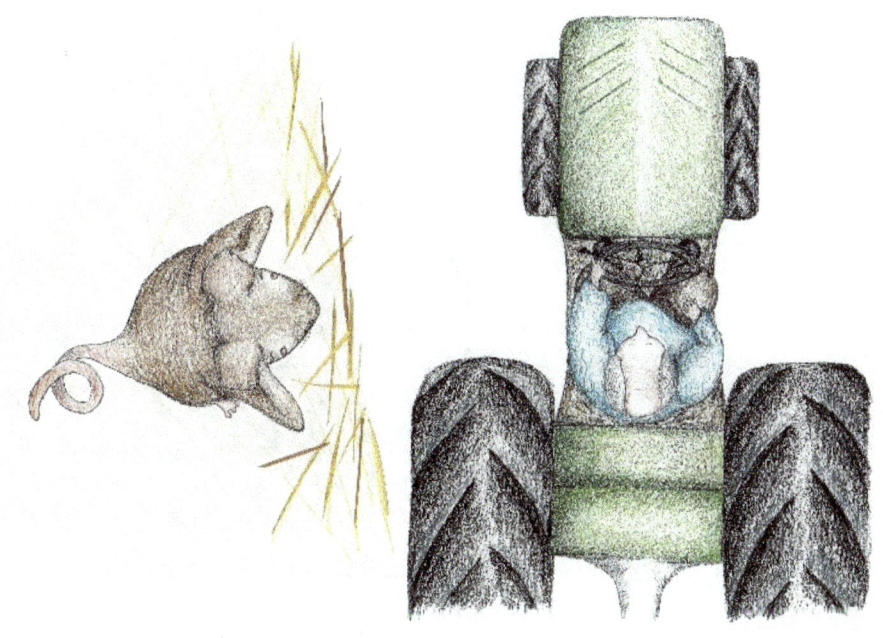

Just then a tractor came by the haystack. There was the loudest rumbly growling and clanking. Noodle felt very scared. He put his paws over his ears. It was more scary than two little brown mouse-ears could listen to.

Noodle lay down on the top hay-bale. The sun shone on him and he got nice and warm. There was so much warm he felt cosy all the way to his insides.

Along came a strong wind. It blew so hard that one of the hay-bales bumped into Noodle and knocked him down the crack between the hay. He fell down and down and down.

Till he landed at the bottom. Where his Auntie Needle, and all his brothers, sisters, and cousins were waiting for him.

"What is God like?" Auntie asked.

"Big," said Noodle, when he remembered the bright blue. "And scary," he said, when he remembered the noise. "And warm," he said, when he remembered the sun.

"And VERY, VERY STRONG !" he said, when he remembered the wind.

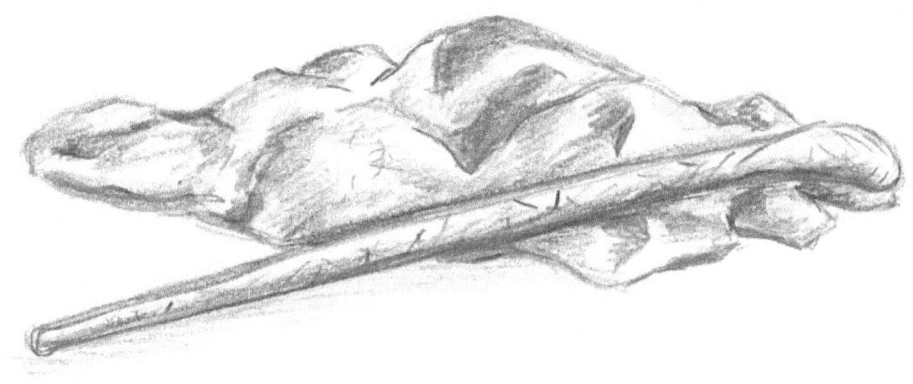

Old Martha

2 Corinthians 5:17

The dawn's light was making its way into Martha's room. More out of habit than necessity she sat up, swung her stiff legs over the side of the bed and painfully got to her feet. Martha prepared to begin her day. She filled the shallow basin with water and washed the sleep from her face. Next she removed her nightdress. For a moment she smoothed her hands across her chest and down to the loose folds of her belly.

She sighed. It had been many years since her Benjamin had found pleasure with her; many more since her body had carried and nurtured their eight children. She scolded herself for such self-indulgent thoughts. She was an old, widowed woman and that was that. Nothing she could do about it. She got dressed.

Soon Martha was settling herself at the small table by the window. She always enjoyed this quiet hour of reading, reflecting, and praying. It felt luxurious to be here. There were chores to be done, to be sure, but no-one but herself would determine when those tasks would happen. That was an advantage of being old, possibly the only one.

Street noises drifted up just as Martha finished her prayers. Something she had been reading filled her thoughts and she continued to ponder on it while cautiously moving from one creaking stair to the next, step by step, down to the room below. The house was old too. Was it the staircase creaking or herself?

Thomas, her grandson, had brought the water jugs in. The broom was there, by the door, and some fresh loaves on the table. All provided by Thomas. Soon her neighbour would call in to ensure Martha had managed to wake up and wasn't lying dead in her bed. Of course she never said that, just made it appear that she was passing by and, well, thought she'd pop in. They would share a pot of tea and village gossip and then Martha would be alone again. How was it that everyone was in a hurry, with more tasks to do than hours in a day to do them? As she swept the floor, cleared the table, and contemplated eating something, Martha watched the street outside. Men pushing carts, small children running, women carrying baskets that would presently be holding their market purchases, a few stray dogs barking, and somewhere, a donkey braying.

Without any forethought Martha suddenly wanted to visit The House, and as quickly as she could she grabbed her shawl and her cane and stepped into the street. Her destination was perhaps half a mile along several busy thoroughfares, which meant she should stay close to the buildings. To venture into the stream of human busyness would be treacherous for an old woman. When she reached Peter's house Martha's breath was coming in short gasps but a moment of leaning against the doorframe allowed it to return to enough of normal. She rang the bell.

Silas opened the door and beamed when he saw her. "I wonder," she enquired of him, "if Mark is here?" "Providence is on your side today," Silas replied, and he ushered her in. He continued, "actually he is not here at this moment, but by the time you have taken some refreshment and recovered from your walk, he will have arrived." Martha wondered if it was so obvious how exhausted she felt. Nevertheless, she was well rested when Mark strode into the room. She didn't hear him approach, her eyes were closed momentarily and she was deep in thought. Maybe even snoring a little!

Soon there were two cups of wine brought to the table and the two friends were reminiscing.

"Our group followed the Teacher everywhere didn't we, Mark?" said Martha. "I am certain we walked the length and breadth of Palestine a hundred times over, and never once was I out of breath!"

Mark nodded. "I'm glad I wrote it all down. People nowadays would not believe the Teacher could have done all that He did. So many miracles, so much teaching. He turned this world on its head."

"Ah yes," agreed Martha. "He turned the Temple on its head, and more."

They both leaned back in their chairs. A little 'saging and aging' occurred. The minutes passed.

Martha broke the silence. "Brother Mark" she said, "do you remember all the miracles and the healings?"

"Well," he answered, giving his mind a moment to recall as much as it could. "A lot, I guess. Perhaps not all …"

"There were the demons He drove out," she offered.

"And sons and daughters He cured of disease." Mark added.

"Remember the man by the pool?"

"And the woman who touched His cloak!"

"Remember that day the man came down through the roof? Wasn't that something."

"What about old Peter's mother-in-law?"

"The blind saw, the lame walked, the deaf could hear!" they both said in unison.

"Yes! But don't forget those people, like Lazarus, who were *dead*, and then raised to life again."

"And Jesus himself rose from the dead!!"

Now they were both almost breathless with the excitement of recollecting.

A long time passed before either of them said more, and again it was Martha who broke the silence.

"Brother Mark," she almost exhaled the words. "Did he ever, do you recall, if he ever *made an old person young again?*"

The two friends gazed into each other's rheumy eyes.

Hours later they were still debating Martha's question. It took them along a myriad theories, timeless truths, and finally, set it down where all of life's hardest questions will be answered. Where the old is gone and all are made new. In Christ.

The Weeniest, Teeniest Seed

A Puppet play for Nick, Benny and Zoe.

Based on Matt. 13:31&32

Nick:	Hey green boy, what you got there?
Benny:	I beg your pardon, but my name is Benny.
Nick:	Cool. Now what's that you're holding?
Benny:	Oh, nothing you'd be interested in. Its just a little seed.

Nick:	*(looks in Benny's hand)* Well that's gotta be the weeniest, teeniest seed in the whole world, Benny. What are you growing? A FLEA?
Benny:	Fleas don't grow from seeds. *(pause)* Hey, what's your name?
Nick:	The name's Nick and I am one cool dude - if you know what I mean.
Benny:	Yeah. Nick's a cool name. Pleased to meet you.
Nick:	Sure thing Button Boy. I gotta go now. Time marches on. Keep a tight grip on that seed!

(Nick leaves and Zoe arrives)

Benny:	Hi Zoe. Did you see that cool dude that just left?
Zoe:	Yeah, that was Nick. *(notices Benny is holding something)* So what are you holding in your hand - your last dollar?
Benny:	Oh Zoe, this is worth more than a dollar. It's a mustard seed. My Dad gave it to me.
Zoe:	You mean if you plant that a jar of mustard will grow out of the ground?
Benny:	No! A WHOLE BIG TREE will grow.
Zoe:	You're kidding me. A TREE from that little seed!
Benny:	Nick said it was the weeniest, teeniest seed in the whole world. But my Dad reckons it will grow into a tree big enough for birds to build nests in.
Zoe:	*(amazed)* A whole big tree. Birds and nests and baby birds?
Benny:	And not just a few birds - lots and lots. It says so - in the Bible.
Zoe:	In the Bible?!! Benny why would it say stuff about a mustard seed growing into a tree in the Bible?

Benny: Well, it's one of those parables …

Zoe: … that Jesus told. I know about them.

Benny: Dad read it to me last night. Jesus said we only need to have a little bit of faith to start with … and it will grow, and grow, and grow …

Zoe: …'til it's as big as a tree!

Benny: But there's still something I don't understand. Maybe Nick would know. He's such a cool dude.

(Nick returns)

Nick: Did I hear someone say my name?

Zoe: Oh hi, Nick! Benny needs help.

Nick: *(turning to Benny)* Well Button Boy, help has arrived!

Benny: Nick, do you know what faith is? You see, in the Bible Jesus tells us to have faith - even a little bit.

Nick: *(thinks for a moment)* It's not easy to explain, but, basically it's believing in Jesus and what He said even if we can't see Him.

Benny: Hey yeah! I get it now. And I think I've got some faith, just a bit. What about you Zoe? Have you got a mustard-seeds-worth of faith?

Zoe: I'm sure I do. *(turns to Nick)* What about you Nick?

Nick: There you go again, talking about seeds.

You two need to explain something to ME!

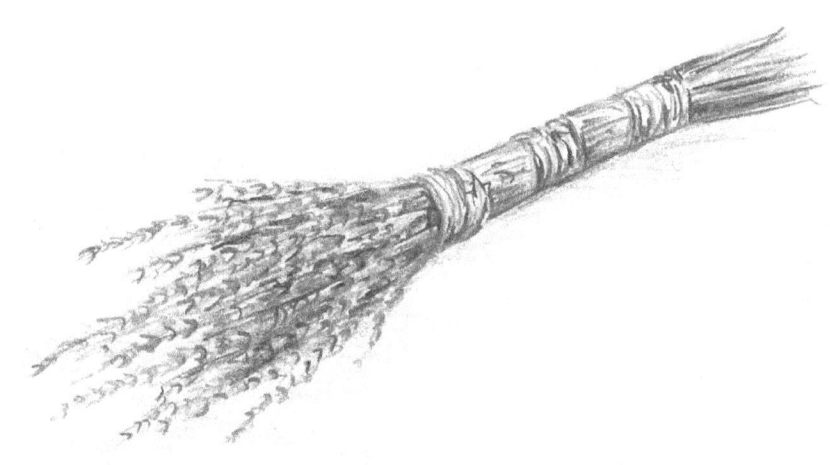

Rachel's Lamb

A retelling of Exodus 12

It had always been Rachel's lamb, right from the moment he was born, almost a year ago. He was so perfect with pure, white wool. Rachel had held him close to her. She had wrapped him in a cloth and watched as he nuzzled next to his mother.

Every day for nearly a year Rachel ran into the field behind their house to check on her special little lamb. How he had grown!

Now Daddy was carrying her lamb into the shed. "What are you doing Daddy?"

"Where are you taking him?"

Slowly Rachel's father put the lamb down and gathered Rachel into his arms.

"Everybody is doing it … It's what God has told us to do … We're going on a long trip … Our family needs your lamb because he is so perfect …"

Daddy's voice was quiet and his face was sad. Rachel felt frightened. "But Daddy … why?"

Rachel suddenly wished her lamb wasn't so perfect. Maybe if he'd had a lame leg, or black flecks through his fleece. She looked down at the woolly sheep nuzzling against her arm. Tears welled up in her eyes. Daddy led her outside.

"Go inside the house. Help your mother bake the bread. Rachel, God has promised that this will be the last sadness for us. Go."

Soon the smell of bread baking filled the house. And there was a stew bubbling on the fire. But no-one was thinking of food.

Rachel and her brothers Simeon and Zerah were packing things into leather bags. Clothes, cooking pots, rope, sandals. She had forgotten about her lamb for a while, but now she saw her father painting something red on their door. It was blood.

Rachel shivered. She ran behind him, tugging at his sleeve. "But Daddy, "she asked again, "why?"

He put the pot down and carefully laid the hyssop-brush alongside.

In the midst of all the hurry and haste, Rachel's Daddy took her on his knee.

"Your little lamb was needed to save us. Yes. God has said we will die when the angel of death comes in the night unless the blood of a little lamb, your perfect little lamb, is painted over the door. Do you understand, my child?"

"Yes, yes. I do understand. My lamb was born especially to save us!" She jumped off her father's lap.

There was no more time to talk. Mother was pushing a bowl of stew in front of Rachel.

"Eat, quick. Eat. Soon we must leave."

Rachel and her family lived long, long ago. God did save his people. They left their homes and escaped from the Egyptians who had ruled over them. For so many years God's people had worked hard for them and had been treated badly. They had been slaves.

Then in one night God led them out and away. They were free!

In the Bible there is another Lamb. He is called the Lamb of God.

Do you know who he is? He is Jesus.

Just like Rachel's family and her people, we were all slaves of sin. That means we couldn't help doing wrong and hating God. We were God's enemies. He wanted us to love Him but we couldn't.

Then God let His Precious Son die so we would escape death. His Son, Jesus, was much more precious than Rachel's lamb, much more loved, and even more perfect.

At Easter we remember when God's Son - The Lamb of God, died on a cross. Jesus was born in a stable and grew to be man just for this day. The Day when He would set us all free to love God.

Are you free? Remember the Lamb.

Stephanie's in Heaven

Luke 18: 15-17

Stephanie opened her eyes and blinked slowly - blink, blink, blink. The room was filled with a wonderful light. Not the kind of light she'd seen before. This was a warm glow that seemed to go right inside her. The warmth of it reminded her of that other place she had been. That wet, weightless world where warmth was part of her existence. Another part was the k-thump, k-thump, k-thump, k-thump - telling her everything was good. This place was good too.

Stephanie kicked her legs around, pushing her toes against the wicker basket that was her baby-bed. It felt nice to do that - testing out those small limbs which would one day take her running along sparkling footpaths and over lush green grass. She laughed and waved her chubby arms about with the sheer joy that filled her heart.

Suddenly the room became brighter still. Two brilliant figures stood close to Stephanie's crib - angels with kindly faces and gentle smiles. They looked down at Stephanie, her arms waving wildly.

"The whole Kingdom of God wrapped up in a tiny baby," said one. The other angel bent over Stephanie and stroked her cheek.

Stephanie closed her eyes. The angel's touch reminded her again of another place, another time. Firm hands - sometimes large and rough, sometimes soft and small - supporting her when she hadn't been weightless. Gentle touches of fingers, lips and even tears against her skin.

Could it be that they were still there and the angel could feel them? Or had they disappeared when she came to this place? Stephanie didn't know. But as she lay there, she knew all those touches, all those precious words whispered in her ears, were with her still. They dwelt deep inside her. They hovered in the warmth of the air around her. They were part of the golden glow.

Nice

A puppet play for Mo, Lizzie, and introducing Zoe.

Based on Acts 16:13- 15

Mo: Lizzie. Lizzie. Lizzie!

(Lizzie arrives)

Lizzie: Hang on Mo. Settle down. I'm right here.

Mo: Lizzie, am I glad to see you. You'll never guess what's happened. Truly Lizzie, you'll never guess. Never in a trillion years.

Lizzie: Okay. Looks like you'll have to tell me. Spit it out Mo.

Mo: (*excited*) There's a new kid around here !

Lizzie: Go on!!?? You mean another P.U.P.P.E.T. (*whispers*)

Mo: Yep. And she's GORGEOUS !

Lizzie: Well I'm not her friend. There's only room here for one girl - and that's ME.

Mo: (*sadly*) What are you going to do to her Lizzie?

Lizzie: Well – I'll pull her hair. (Mo: Ouch!) Then I'll head-butt her. (Mo: Ouch!) Then I'll chase her down the corridor and scream at her to GET LOST!!

Mo: But she might be nice.

Lizzie: Won't ever find out. There's no room around here for HER!

Mo: But she might be really, really nice.

Lizzie: No-one could be as nice as me. *(Zoe enters. Lizzie doesn't see her)* Now show me where she is and I'll get rid of her!!!

Mo: *(clears throat)* Hurruph Hurrum. She's right here, Lizzie.

Lizzie: *(spins around to see Zoe. Sweetly ...)* Well, hello there. You must be the new girl. I'm Lizzie.

Zoe: Hello Lizzie. My name's Zoe. It's so nice of you to welcome me to your neighbourhood.

Mo: Yeah well ... Lizzie was just saying she is the nicest girl around here. 'Course we don't know what you're like yet.

Lizzie *(looks Zoe over)* She looks nice to me.

Mo:	Maybe she's like Lydia. You remember that lady in the Bible that made everyone feel welcome and was kind to strangers. *(Aside to Lizzie)* Hey Lizzie you could take a few lessons from her!
Zoe:	I know about Lydia. She was a friend of Paul at the time when the Church was just starting. Way back in the Year Dot.
Lizzie:	With Adam and Eve and The Snake?
Zoe:	No, not that Year Dot. About twenty years after Jesus went back to Heaven.
Lizzie:	Let's just say it was a long time ago.
Zoe:	It was on one of Paul's preaching trips. This lady - Lydia, was living in a town he visited. She believed in God and while she was listening to Paul, God worked in her heart.
Mo:	Is that when she decided to be loving and kind?
Zoe:	Yes. It was when she decided to believe what Paul said about Jesus coming, and dying, and rising from the grave. After she believed all that, she invited Paul and his friends to her house.
Lizzie:	And that was a kind and loving thing to do.
Mo:	So, once we ask Jesus into our hearts, we want to be different? We become nicer people?
Zoe:	Yeah, that's what you two were talking about when I got here. Being nice.
Lizzie:	I think we could all work at becoming nicer people.
Mo:	Especially you Lizzie! No more pulling hair and head-butting!
Lizzie:	Yeah, yeah. Okay.

Story for Rohan

A retelling of John 6:1- 13

Simeon's face was screwed up, worry-lines across his forehead.

What did his Dad think he was doing, just deciding in a moment to go off with the crowd to listen to that drifter, Jesus.

Now Simeon would have to make sure they had everything for a day's outing. Quickly he grabbed a satchel. While his mother swept the floor, Simeon looked around for a few provisions – it might be a long day! Again he thought - *What was his father thinking of?* Papa was a hard worker, doing whatever came his way. Right now he had a job helping the fishermen. He was mending nets, cleaning the catch, or repairing the small fishing boats. Not turning up for work today might mean the end of that job. And with Mama always being sick … sometimes Simeon thought he was the only person in the family with any sense! At least they had him to get things done.

"Where is that boy?" He heard Papa call. "Hurry son, the crowd is almost out of town." Simeon scooped up an armful of the little white rolls Mama had just taken out of the oven. Then he saw a basket of fish on the table. Before his mother turned, he grabbed a couple - one for him, one for Papa.

"Hey there Simeon, what have you got?" Mama yelled after him as he bolted out of the door. "Just a bite of lunch, Mama. I love you!"

As he ran after his father, Simeon was still stuffing the rolls into the satchel.

"This will be a wonderful day," Papa was saying to a neighbour, also on the trip. "Too good for working. Did you know, this man Jesus? He says he is the Messiah. So many of the fishermen have left their nets to follow Him - permanently! So I say - what is just one day? Surely, they won't sack a man for listening to the Messiah."

Simeon's brow wrinkled again. That worried look was back. He wondered how the family would manage without Papa's wage. He worried about whether Papa would find another job. Suddenly he saw his friends ahead. He ran to catch them. He was a good, fast runner - everybody said so. Soon all other thoughts had vanished. Like Papa had said, this will be a wonderful day.

The crowd was very large, it seemed as if the whole countryside was here. The men were at the front, listening to Jesus. Simeon and his friends played together a little way off. First they played tag, then hide-and-seek. Wherever Simeon went or whatever he did, Papa would be watching him. Or that's what Simeon thought. Every so often he would hear – 'Simeon, stay away from that ditch or tree, or well.' *Did Papa think he couldn't look after himself?*

Simeon and his friends found some sticks and some twine. They decided to make a pen, like a sheep pen. Simeon was good at making things. He told the other boys how to poke the sticks into the ground and attach the twine. Then he ran to his father and, while Papa was listening very carefully so that his mouth hung open at something Jesus was saying, Simeon popped his hand inside his father's coat and took his knife from his belt. "Hey son!" His father called just as he turned, "You behaving well?"

"Oh yes Papa," Simeon lied.

When he got back to his friends he pulled out the knife.

"Ooo Simeon, are you old enough to have a knife?" "Yes!" he said, "and I know how to use it too."

And so with the knife held like he'd seen his father hold it, Simeon tried to carve one of the sticks. "I'll make some little sheep for the pen. Lots of sheep. You'll see," he said to them. But he wasn't sure how it was to be done. The knife didn't move the way it did in Papa's old brown hands.

"Let's play tag again," his friends called.

The sun was high in the sky. Simeon was getting hungry. He put the knife into his pocket and followed the other boys.

Now there was a man walking through the crowd. Many people were sitting or lying on the grass. It was hot in the sun and lunchtime had already passed, un-noticed. "Have you brought food?" he was calling.

No-one said anything. A few shook their heads, some said something about seeing miracles.

Simeon thought proudly, "*At least I have some lunch for Papa and me. That's because I'm smart enough to think of these things before I start out for the day!*" But deep inside a voice reminded him there were other things he was not able to take care of. Like Papa losing his job and Mama being sick. His worried face returned. "Mister," he yelled. "Mister, I have some food. I thought to bring some for my Papa and me. But you can have it. It's not a lot."

The man came over to Simeon. "Well," he said, looking into the satchel. "We'll see what the Master says."

Simeon ran along beside the man, up the hill to Jesus.

"This boy has a little lunch," the man told Jesus, who took it from him. Simeon plopped himself down in front of them, waiting to see whether Jesus would eat his lunch or share a bit with him. After all, Simeon had been smart enough to think of it. Not even Jesus had packed any food.

Slowly Jesus took a little of the bread roll. As He turned towards the crowd the people fell quiet. Jesus looked over the crowd, then up to the sky. With the bright sun shining on His upturned face, He blessed Simeon's lunch. Then He began to hand out the loaves and fishes.

Right before his eyes Simeon saw people everywhere break off CHUNKS, and stuff them into their mouths.

"Mmm, Mmm. These are good fish!" he heard them say.

"Compliments to the woman who baked this bread!" one man said, and others mumbled in agreement as they ate more and more.

Simeon was astonished! He looked back at Jesus who was looking right at him. He beckoned to Simeon. Simeon got up and went to Jesus who put his arm across Simeon's shoulder.

"You are a good boy to think of things like food, and your family, - your Papa's job and your Mama's illness. But Simeon, did you notice today that I took care of all these people's hunger? I will always look after my sheep because I am the Good Shepherd."

Then Jesus kneeled down and put His fingers on Simeon's forehead. He gently smoothed away the wrinkles on his brow. Then He passed His hands over Simeon's face.

"Go," He said, "and never worry again. I AM taking care of everything."

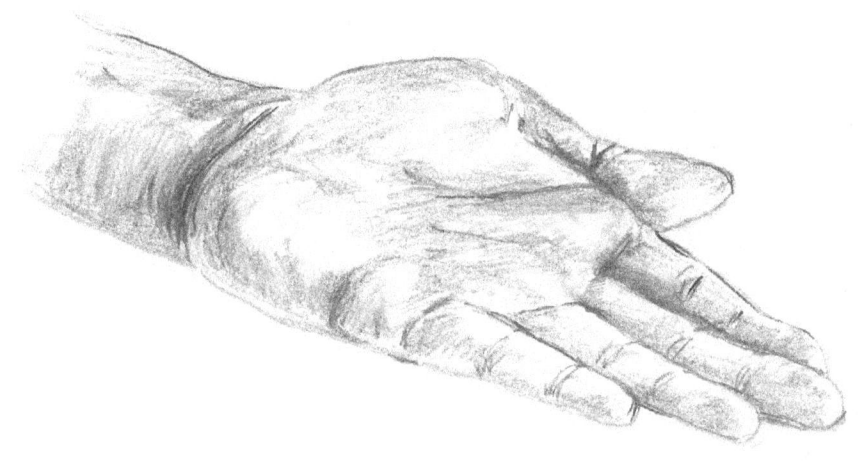

The Invisible Man

A reflection on Matt 12:1-14

Mostly I am ignored at the temple. I go every week to pay my tithe, say my prayers, listen to the priest's words, and no-one seems to notice me – I'm invisible.

Imagine my surprise when Jesus, surrounded by his followers *and* a gaggle of Pharisees, marched right up to me. Me! An invisible man with a shrivelled hand, who no-one ever wants to see, let alone help.

They were arguing about something. Arguing politely, but I could tell that those lawyers were trying to trap Jesus with his own words.

They stopped before me.

"Is it lawful to heal on the Sabbath?" they asked him.

Ah, so I was their visual aid. Here was a "rubber meets the road" moment for Jesus. Or should that be "donkey's foot pad meets the road?"

Well, he answered the question with a question. And then using the convenience of a man in need of a miracle close by, Jesus drove his point home. "Stretch out your hand," he told me. I did. I gazed down at my hands. They were both as perfect as each other!

Heavenly father,

It is not the rules that keep us right with you. It is not what we give up or do without. You only want us to live "mercifully"; to value our fellow humans as you do; to do good, every day of every week. Help me go through this life journey following Jesus in all that I do.

Amen.

Star Gazing

A puppet play for Mo and Lizzie

Begins with Mo looking skyward

Lizzie: Hey, Mo. Whatcha doin'?

Mo: Looking at the stars, Lizzie. There are so many of them. I was counting them but now I've lost count - thanks to you!

Lizzie: Gee you're dumb Mo. There are too many stars to count them.

Mo: But I was reading about how Abraham in the Bible had as many children as the stars in the sky.

Lizzie: WOW! *(She's impressed. Then ...)* Nah! I remember Abraham in the Bible. He had only one kid - Isaac. ONE kid, Mo. And he was no star!

Mo: You always think you know better. But this time ... I'M RIGHT!

God took Abraham into the night. He said to Abraham, "Look up Abe. See all those twinkly stars?"

Lizzie: And Abraham said, "Yeah ..."

Mo: Yep! Then God said, "You will have as many children as there are stars. I PROMISE."

Lizzie: Like a whole tribe of people?

Mo: Exactly! God said it would be a nation. A great big nation of God's people. Thousands, Millions, Trillions

Lizzie: Wow! That's AWESOME *(pause)* Hey, Mo?

Mo: Yeah?

Lizzie: Why? Why did Abraham, why did God want a whole nation of people?

Mo: Well, He wanted to bless them so they could be a blessing to the world.

Lizzie: Mo, I think you are smarter than me. What's a blessing?

Mo: It's when we do good stuff for each other. God was going to do some really good stuff for the whole world. He was going to bring along Jesus to save us.

Lizzie: Ah, Jesus! I was wondering when we would get to Him.

Mo:	Well Abraham, Isaac, and all their kids, grandkids, great, great grandkids… You know - that whole nation, would eventually get to the one who would be Jesus - the SAVIOUR.
Lizzie:	So, Jesus is one of Abraham's children?
Mo:	*(Thinking)*
	I guess so.
	All part of God's plan, remember?
Lizzie:	Yeah, Yeah, I get it.
	God made a promise, and he kept it.

The Parable of the Lost Lego Block

A Retelling of Luke 14,15 and thereabouts

Now supposing one of you had three hundred and twenty-nine thousand, five hundred and seventy-six LEGO blocks: Red, black, blue, yellow and white. Long skinny ones, small squarish ones, flat ones, sloping roof ones, blocks with hinges and blocks with little window bits in them. Mmmmm … it makes your heart beat a little faster, doesn't it?

Suppose one of you has all these LEGO blocks and supposing that one of you wants to build a tower. Will he not first sit down and estimate the cost to see if he has enough bricks to complete it?

Well, yes he will.

But what if that "one of you" knows all his LEGO blocks intimately? What if he knows he has one thousand, two hundred and seventy blue roof blocks and one hundred blue corner roof pieces?

When that man comes to building the roof of his tower he will count on all those pieces being there. Confidently he will build higher, higher, higher. The roof will move upwards beautifully, towards a perfect peak …

And then. Oh No! Disaster!

Quickly that man will count the corner roof blocks already used … 96, 97, 98, 99 … NO MORE!

Frantically that man will tip his tower upside down and shake it. (Sometimes a block will fall inside while you're building.) But no, nothing there.

Carefully that man will check the other blocks lying around. He will count all of them - thirteen thousand, five hundred and sixty-three small squarish blocks, nine thousand, nine hundred and eighty-one long skinny ones, six hundred and eighty-five with little window bits … AND ONLY NINETY-NINE BLUE CORNER ROOF BLOCKS!

"Kids!" he will call, "one of my roof blocks is lost!"

And they come running. They light a lamp and sweep every corner of the house. That man cannot rest until he finds his lost LEGO block. And then, when despair and grief have almost exhausted him, (and the rest of the family), that man finds his blue corner roof block!

He puts his lost LEGO block on his shoulder and carries it home.

He goes to his neighbours and friends and says, "Come rejoice with me for I have found my lost LEGO block!"

Ah! what joy that will be. You see all that man's neighbours love LEGO blocks as much as he. The lady across the street even bakes him a celebration cake in the shape of a LEGO block.

Well Jesus told lots of 'lost and found' stories and he might have told this one too, if they had LEGO blocks back then. He wanted us to know that when precious things are lost – we're sad. And when they are found – we're happy.

And when one of His precious children (you and me) is found and comes to Him, He throws a party in heaven. Every time someone says to Jesus "I believe you love me" and really means it, everyone in heaven, angels and all, have a big celebration.

Maybe they've had a party for you. Or maybe they will have one soon.

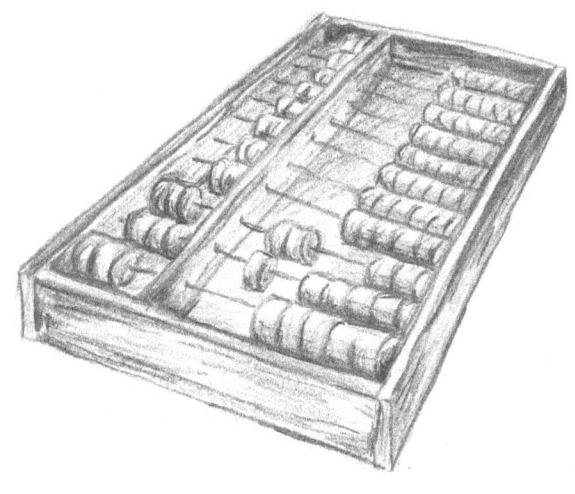

The Man on the Ground

Reimagining Ezekiel 4

Week Two

He is still there. Ben and Jake walk past on the other side of the street but they never take their eyes off him. "That is seriously weird!" whispers Ben. Jake nods in agreement. "Come on, we'll be late for classes," he says, and they both hurry towards the House.

The man on the ground has been there for a week or so. It's not just the man though, it's the stuff he has with him. A clay tile and what looks like an army of toy soldiers and miniature ramps around it. And, most peculiar of all, an iron plate that he holds up between himself and the toys. To one side there's a small brazier with a pot. It smells funny, nasty funny.

At midday the brothers return. Once again, they stare at the man reclining uncomfortably on the roadside.

Week Six

"He never moves! He's just there, in the same position every day, and I don't know why," Ben tells his mother. "What's he doing?"

"Nobody knows. He's a prophet who thinks God is talking to him." She takes the leather satchel from him. "Nothing for you to worry about."

Week Twelve

Jake holds his older brother's hand but he deliberately slows their progress by sliding his feet in the gravel road, rather than lifting them. Ben is getting annoyed. "What's with you today? Hurry up!"

"I want to talk with him." That's all Jake says but his brother knows exactly who he means. And he lets go of Jake's hand. The younger boy crosses the road and approaches the man. Ben watches from the other side.

Week Fourteen

Every day Jake sits beside Ezekiel, while Ezekiel maintains his pose of lying on his left side, holding a metal plate between himself and the clay tile. It's become a ritual for the boy. He now knows who the man is and something of why he is doing this bizarre charade. It frightens him. He gazes at the ropes holding the prophet and wonders who tied him up. Who?

Week Twenty

Yesterday an angry crowd had gathered near Ezekiel when Ben and Jake made their way to their classes. The prone man spoke his message from God in calm tones but he needn't have bothered. They understood the meaning of the tile with a sketch of Jerusalem on it. They could see the 'city' was under siege from the ramps around it. And they knew what it meant when the Man of God held an iron plate against their city.

Week Thirty

"Is this all you could buy for our meal?" Ben and Jake's father asks his wife one evening. "Rations, I'm afraid. I'm only allowed to buy our portion." She says.

Their father continues, "It's that crackpot preacher who's behind this. The one lying in the street. It's embarrassing to have that constant reminder right under our noses. Really, what does he expect us to do?"

It was a question spoken without the need of an answer but Jake answered it anyway. "Repent" he said. "Come back to God."

His father had a swift reply. "God? What has God done for us lately? Maybe it would be better to worship the other gods. See if they can put food on our table?"

Week Forty

Ben has joined Jake sitting beside Ezekiel. The prophet speaks freely to them, describing his life before Yahweh told him to lie down; of the other strange things God has commanded him to do. "Can you imagine what The Scroll tastes like?" he asks the lads one day. They both shake their heads. "Honey" says Ezekiel. "The Words of God were harsh and bitter and yet, it tasted like honey!" He uses one hand to hold the plate while rubbing his eyes with the other. "And still the people don't turn back."

Week Fifty

"How long did God say you had to stay here?" Ben asks Ezekiel.

"Three hundred and ninety days," replies the prophet. "One day for every year of the people's sin against God." The two boys before him shudder. "But there is worse to come."

Week Fifty-five

Ben is ready for classes early. He knows what today is: the end of the siege! "It's over," he shouts to his younger brother, and Jake is up and dressed in no time. Soon they're running towards the man lying on the ground.

"You can get up now!" Jake announces before they have even crossed the street.

But the prophet doesn't move. Ben stares, trying to understand. Seeing that Ezekiel has already moved from the position of the past fifty-five weeks, the boys drop to their knees beside him. Jake puts his arm around the man's shoulders as tears streak down his face. "What?" Ben asks, bewildered.

Because Ezekiel is now lying on his right side.

Note

You can find the story of Ezekiel in the Bible. (Ezekiel chapter 4 is about the sieges described here.) Perhaps you are intrigued to read the whole of the biblical account.

I wonder why God told Ezekiel to lie down on his side. I wonder what you would think if you saw a Man of God doing such strange things. I wonder if you would listen.

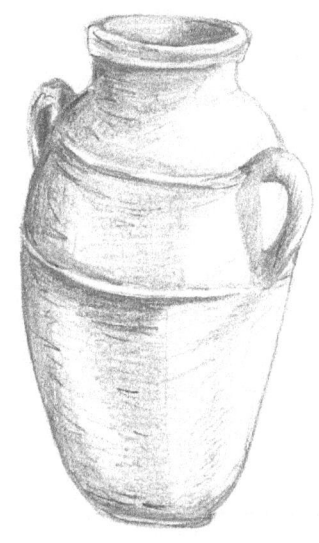

The Wedding at Cana

A reflection on John 2:1-11

I surely must have had as much to drink as those around me, and the celebrations are set to continue for a while yet. On observing Jesus taking his mother to task and giving strange orders to the servants, my interest was piqued. How amazing the resulting miracle! Who is this man? Who is he related to? Where can I find out more about him?

To follow Jesus at this point would be to follow a magician, a sideshow. What about when he begins to say things people don't want to hear? What about when he starts to make demands of me?

Lord,

May I grow in my understanding of Jesus day by day. Please give me the faith and courage, not just to know him, but also to follow him, willingly, in obedience.

Amen

Put a Smile on God's face

A puppet play for Lizzie and Mo

Mo: Hi Lizzie. It's been a long time since we've been here with the kids at children's church.

Lizzie: Yeah, I think they've forgotten who we are. *(to kids)* Hey kids, what's my name?

(wait for kids to respond)

Mo: Nope. They'll never forget you, Lizzie. You're one out of the box!

Lizzie:	Now Mo – don't make fun of my home. It might be humble but it's the only home I've got.
Mo:	Sorry Lizzie. Hey, I've got a riddle for you.
Lizzie:	Oh Mo I love riddles. Especially yours. Does it come from the Bible?
Mo;	Well sort of. I made it up myself. Ready?
Lizzie:	*(excited)* GO, Go, Go !!!!!!
Mo;	*(clears his throat)* What word makes Mums happy, Dads smile, teachers skip for joy, makes politicians try harder, little kids dance, makes people dig deeper to give, gives warm fuzzies to everyone, makes the angels in heaven sigh, and puts the hugest smile on God's dial?????
Lizzie:	*(shocked)* 'Scuse me, Mo - Did you say - "on God's DIAL"?
Mo:	You know - on His FACE. Puts the hugest smile on God's FACE!
Lizzie:	*(thinking)* Well let me see ... I get pretty happy about lollipops ... but my Dad doesn't like them ... and angels probably never even tasted them ...
Mo:	You're not even warm Lizzie. Keep guessing.
Lizzie:	LOVE!!! Everyone gets excited about love. Is that it?
Mo:	You're getting warmer.
Lizzie:	Give me a clue. Just a little clue.
Mo:	Okay. Let's pretend your Mum brings home a bag of lollipops for you. No-one else can have one. They're all yours. What would you do?
Lizzie:	Go up to my room and eat them, of course.
Mo:	Aw, Lizzie! You're not thinking smart today! I'll give you another clue. Let's pretend

	your Dad does all your chores for you - feeds the cat - sets the table - puts out the garbage - sweeps the front porch. What would you SAY?
Lizzie:	Well, that's easy. I'd say – 'Dad you're wonderful. You're the best Dad a kid could have.'
Mo:	And what else?
Lizzie:	I'd jump around, do a little dance, hug him and …
Mo:	And …
Lizzie:	I'd say 'THANKYOU, THANKYOU, THANKYOU!!!'
Mo:	You got it!! That's the answer to the riddle.
Lizzie:	*(thinking)* Oh yeah. It is too! 'Thankyou' - the word that makes Mums happy, Dads smile, kids dance and puts a smile on God's face. WOW!
Mo:	Everyone likes to be thanked Lizzie. It makes the people who say it feel good and it makes the people who are thanked feel happy too.
Lizzie:	And it makes you feel appreciated, so you try to do more stuff for people. But why does God smile when we say thankyou?
Mo:	He likes to hear us say thankyou to Him for what He's done, but He also wants us to be thankful to each other. It shows we really care about others.
Lizzie:	There's only one thing I can say about all that. Thank you for telling me that riddle.
Mo:	And thank you Lizzie for figuring it out!
Lizzie:	Thank you Mo.
Mo:	No … thank you!
Lizzie:	I really like that word!

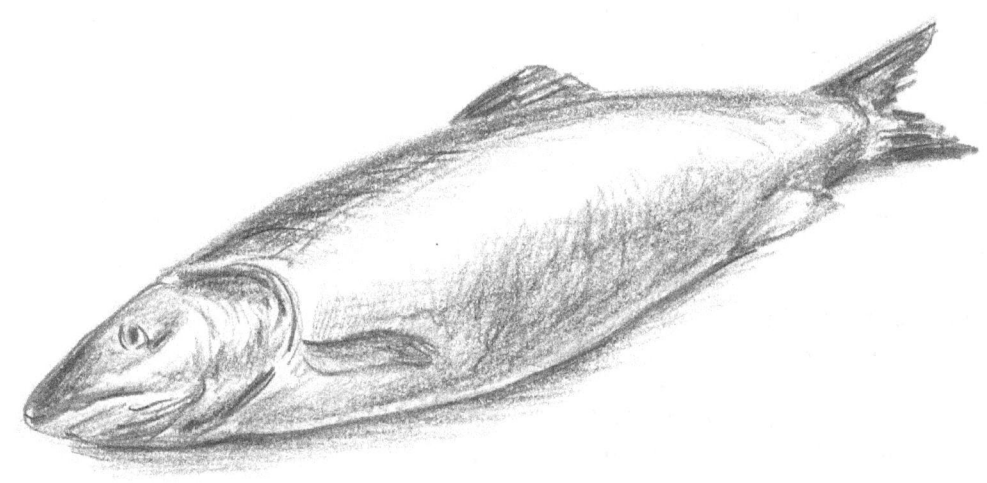

Tom's Fishing Lesson

A story about John 11: 25,26

Tom and Pip were off to the pier. It was school holidays and Tom was going to get a fishing lesson from his friend, Pip.

Pip wasn't an ordinary friend for a boy to have. You see, Pip was a pelican.

Tom first met Pip when he got out of bed one day and stumbled out to the loo. It was a warm, summer morning. He plodded down the hallway and out the backdoor with nothing on but a pair of jocks. Rubbing his eyes and scratching his head, Tom suddenly stopped in his tracks.

There in front of him was a big white flapping creature.

"Mum! Muuuummmmm!" He screamed, turning and running back inside. "Mum! There's this big thing outside. It wants to EAT ME!"

Tom's Mum didn't come. Maybe she was already up at the shops. Tom slumped to the kitchen floor. What was he going to do?

Sooner or later he would have to go outside, because he had to go. I mean he had to go to the LOO, didn't he?

He crawled over to the kitchen window and slowly stood up. The flapping thing was still out there. It was looking right at him. It was TALKING to him!

Well, thought Tom, *how scary can it be? It wasn't all that big. And it had stopped flapping. Now its beak was moving.* Tom thought he'd better go outside to hear what it was saying.

Once again he went out the backdoor and down the path - except now he was wide awake. He looked into the creature's eyes - they were beady black and twinkled.

"I hope I didn't frighten you too much," it said.

"Nah! I had to tell my Mum something," Tom replied.

"My name is Pelican Pip but my friends just call me Pip. Who are you?" Tom wasn't sure about talking pelicans but he answered Pip's question. "I'm Tom … and I'm BUSTING!" he yelled as he bolted to the loo.

Once inside he carefully went over in his mind what just happened. *A talking pelican called Pip?*

He must have been dreaming. That's what it was - a bad dream. There was a knocking on the wall beside him.

"Hey Tom. When are you coming out of there?" "Inaminute …" Tom yelled back. Then he added, "Go away. You're just a dream!"

But when he opened the door, the bird was still there.

"I'm going down to the water and when I come back you're going to be gone," he announced, and went into the house to get his shorts on.

But when he reached the lake, Pip was there on the pier.

"Where's your rod, Tom? I was hoping for a fresh-caught fish for breaky."

"Well, you're out of luck," Tom replied. Then he stopped himself. *This was stupid - talking to a talking pelican. Except that it was really happening.* "Okay," he said, resigning himself, "You're a pelican, and I don't know how, but you talk."

"Does that mean we can be friends?" Pip asked.

"Yeah, but I don't do fishing."

That was yesterday. Pip had wandered along the shore with Tom, telling him things about pelicans and fish. And flying, and fish.

Tom had never met anyone who could talk so much about fish. And before he went home, Tom had agreed to come for this fishing lesson today.

Dad's fishing rod was propped up in the corner of the shed. On the bench was the tackle-box. Tom's Dad never went fishing but he had all the equipment. He grabbed both things and headed towards the lake, meeting Pip along the way. He still sometimes had trouble believing Pip was real. That a pelican could talk. And that he could be such a wonderful friend.

"The pier's the best place to drop your line, Tom." Pip told him. "I'll just buzz around to see where the fish are."

Tom watched as Pip went - half running, half waddling along the shore towards the water. His huge wings flapped wildly about, trying to get Pip airborne. Just when Tom thought his friend would crash into the water, Pip soared into the sky. Changing in an instant from a clumsy creature into a most graceful bird.

Tom reached the end of the pier and put the rod and tackle-box down. Pip was making a few low fly-pasts, peering into the water.

Then he came back alongside the pier. His landing was perfect, touching his feet onto the water and gliding to a stop. He tucked his wings in close to his body and bobbed up and down with the waves.

"Well," he called up to Tom, "there's plenty of fish. Let's catch a few!" He waddled out and came up on to the pier.

Following Pip's directions, Tom soon had the line over the side and in the water. "What happens now?" he asked.

"We just wait for a nibble," Pip said. It didn't take long.

"Pull it in! Pull it in!" shouted Pip. "Reel, reel, faster, faster."

Tom reeled as fast as he could. The fish wriggled about on the hook. Tom let it drop onto the pier. It flapped and jiggled and squirmed and then lay very still. Tom stared at the fish for a long time. Suddenly he started to cry. "It's dead!" he screamed. "I killed it!" Pip couldn't believe what was happening.

"Hey Tom, that's the idea." he tried to tell him. But Tom wasn't listening. Tom was doing something VERY STRANGE!

He had picked up the limp fish and held it close to his chest.

"Oh, poor fishy, I didn't mean for you to be dead," he said and looked into the fish's staring eyes. "I know Pip, he's just pretending, he's just asleep." Tom held the fish by the tail and smacked it hard against the railing - one, two times. Still, it stared blankly back at Tom.

Then Tom put the fish up close to his face. Without hesitating he put his mouth over the fish's mouth, and blew. Nothing happened. Tom tried it again. Finally, he dropped the fish and slumped down next to it.

"It's dead Pip," he said, sadly. "It's dead and nothing will make it alive again."

Tom's fishing lesson reminds me of Jesus. You see, Jesus CAN make dead things alive again. In the Bible God tells us that when we were full of sin we were dead. We were good for nothing. And no-one would ever be able to make us good, any more than Tom could blow life into the fish.

No-one except Jesus. And He did. He took away our sin and gave us new life. Are you dead or alive? Ask Jesus to take away the badness in your heart, then you will live forever.

Is God Grumpy?

A puppet play for Benny and Nick.

Nick: *(mumbling to himself)* I don't want to go! I don't want to go! I don't want to go!

Benny: Hi Nick, You ready to come to church?

Nick: *(shouting angrily)* NO!! I don't want to go to church EVER!

Benny: Aw Nick, You can't say that! My Mum says we should go to church to worship God.

Nick: Why should I go to church? God is just grumpy. He doesn't even like me.

Benny:	*(shocked)* Well ... well ... *(he's lost for words)* Nick, I don't think you can say that.
Nick:	Why not?
Benny:	Well ... it's not true. God is not grumpy.
Nick:	He is too. The Bible says God is like a father, and my Dad is always telling me I'm no good and can't do things properly. I can't even sit in church without fidgeting. If my Dad gets grumpy about that, then God must be really grumpy. After all, it's His church.
Benny:	*(nearly convinced)* Maybe that's true ... no, it can't be! The Bible says God loves us very much - we make Him joyful and ...
Nick:	... oh Benny, that's a joke!! Where does it say that God is joyful about Nick the Puppet?
Benny:	*(speaking to the kids)* I think I need a little help here ... *(spots a leader)* Hey, can you please give me a hand? Have you got a Bible? Please find the verse that says God is pleased about us.
Leader:	In Genesis God said that He was pleased with everything He created - including people.
Benny:	Hmmmm ... anything else?
Leader:	Zephaniah chapter 3 verse 17?
Benny:	That's the one.
Leader:	*(reads out)* "... the LORD will take delight in you, He will sing and be joyful over you, as joyful as people at a festival."
Nick:	You mean God is really HAPPY to see me?

Benny:	ECSTATIC, Nick.
Nick:	Big word Benny. I take it that means joyful?
Benny:	Yeah. God isn't grumpy at all. He is joyful about all of us. He likes to see us, and likes us to laugh and have fun.
Nick:	*(impressed)* WOW!
Benny:	God made the entire world just for us to enjoy. When He watches us have a good time it pleases Him. Actually, God is probably rejoicing when He sees you in church.
Nick:	Even when I can't sit still?
Benny:	Yeah, sure Nick, Even when you're fidgeting. Now come on, get your shoes on. We're outta here!!
Nick:	*(looks up)* See you in church ... *(to Benny)*
	Hey, wait for me, I'm gonna make God laugh.

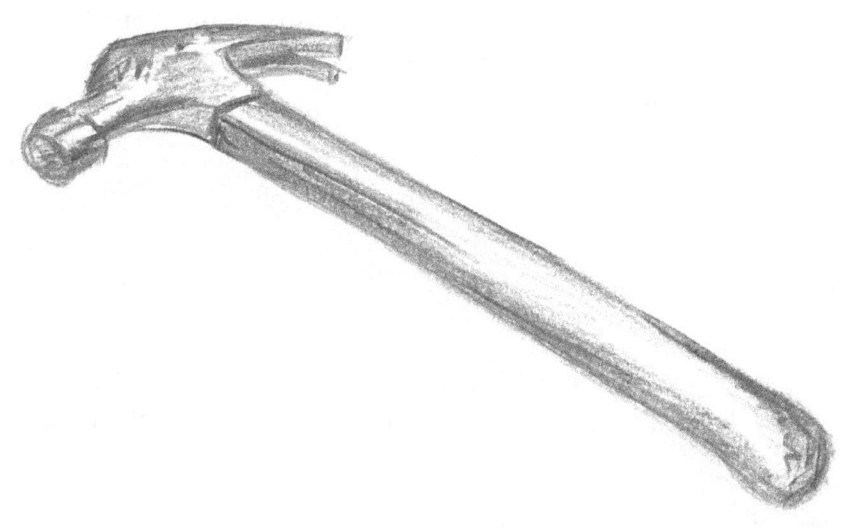

Two Chippies

Matthew 7:24-27, Luke 6:46-49

There were, once upon a time, two builders. One was Pete and the other was Jack.

They were fine, clever people who knew how to build fine, sturdy houses.

Pete was best at walls. He built wooden walls, concrete walls, and brick walls. Sometimes someone would ask him to build a steel wall. No problem. He was good at them all. Pete was so good at building walls he sometimes forgot to first build a good strong floor. He thought to himself, "I can put down just an ordinary sort of floor because my excellent walls will make up for it".

Now Jack was an expert on roofs. Any colour, any design. Tin roofs, tiled roofs, shingled or thatched. Even Colorbond! Sometimes, though, she wasn't so careful about the houses under her roofs. Sometimes the walls were ever so slightly bent. Sometimes the slope of the floor was more of a slope than it should be. "Oh well," thought Jack, "at least the roof is the very best."

One day both these fine builders had the same idea. To build a house for themselves and their family. What a wonderful idea! It would be the grandest house in Geelong. "It will have the most magnificent roof," thought Jack about her new house. "It will have the most splendid walls," thought Pete about his. They both imagined that people would come from far and wide to see their wonderful homes.

The next week they began looking for suitable piece of land to build on. Pete went off towards North Geelong and Jack headed for South Geelong. That night they told their family, "I've found just the perfect spot!"

And it wasn't long before those houses were coming along nicely. Jack's house was long - a house with a lot of roofs. Pete's house was high (in some places) and low (in other places). It had many, many rooms with many, many walls. Each house truly was magnificent. A beautiful and sturdy building.

But there was one very important difference between Pete's house and Jack's.

Pete liked sand. He loved to go to the beach and play with the stuff. He liked the feel of it between his toes. So of course, he chose to build his house close to the beach - right on the sand in fact. Once he moved in, he enjoyed opening his front door, sniffing the salty sea smells and stepping right onto the warm sand. It oozed between his toes, and then he'd get down and build a sandcastle, right there near the door.

Jack wasn't so keen on sand. And she saw right away that it might not be a good place to build a house. Her new house stood on land that was high and solid rock. Some people had said it wasn't such a good idea but Jack brought in big drills and bolted the house down so securely in the rock that nothing would ever shift it. She enjoyed opening her front door, looking over the roofs of the city below, and then stamping her foot on the solid rock beneath her. It hurt, but it sure made her feel safe.

After a few weeks of Pete's sand-oozing and Jack's foot-stamping, a big storm blew in across the bay. The sky turned black with storm clouds, the hailstones pelted down, and the wind blew hard. Pete felt okay. "My walls will stand against this fearsome fury." And Jack felt okay. "My roof will hold up against these giant hail-stones."

But it kept on raining and raining. The wind kept blowing and blowing. Lightning and thunder came closer.

Pete felt his house move just a bit. He ran outside and saw that the sea was rising. The sandcastles by his front door were collapsing in the rain. The sand was very wet and it was shifting! And then, in just a few short moments, the whole building caved in. Down came the roof, down came all the walls. Smashed!

Jack's house was also being battered by the storm. The wind blew hard against her walls. The rain pelted onto her roof and raced along the guttering and downpipes. She wondered if the walls (slightly bent), and the floor (slightly sloping), could stand against the storm. Then she remembered the rock under her feet. She stamped her foot as she thought about it. Why, the whole house- walls and floor and roof - was bolted into that rock.

Jesus told this parable to the people. His word is the Rock.

Do You Recognise Me?

A puppet play for Mo and Lizzie

(n.b. Mo is a green puppet with red hair and little brain.)

Lizzie: Wow Mo! You don't look so good.

Mo: I wouldn't know how I look, Lizzie.

Lizzie: You should take a look in the mirror. You look kinda green around the edges.

Mo: I've never seen a mirror. What do they do?

Lizzie: If you've never seen a mirror, then how would you recognise yourself?

Mo:	Lizzie, I don't need to recognise myself. I know who I am!
Lizzie:	Hey Mo. Wanna hear a story from the Bible. It's about nine guys who didn't recognise Jesus.
Mo:	Anyone would know who Jesus was. He had blond hair, a beard, and he wore a long white dress.
Lizzie:	That's not funny Mo.
Mo:	Okay Liz – Hit me with the facts.
Lizzie:	Well, there were once these ten men. And they were really sick with some dreadful skin disease - like chicken pox, measles, sun burn and itchy bites all at once. No-one would go near them. They were YUK!
Mo:	More than just green around the edges, huh?
Lizzie:	Yeah, maybe green all over!
Mo:	*(disgusted)* OOOooooooo!
Lizzie:	Then Jesus comes down the road. They know he's some teacher or something, and they've heard that he can heal people. So they ask him to make them well again.
Mo:	And he did!
Lizzie:	Hang on. Not so quick! Jesus told them, "Go and show yourselves to the priests." While they were going there the skin disease disappeared.
Mo:	I bet they were happy about that.
Lizzie:	Well, they were ALL happy to be better, but only ONE came back to Jesus. You wanna know why?
Mo:	Yep!

Lizzie:	Because that one man knew WHO Jesus was.
Mo:	Blond hair, beard, white robe … had to be Jesus!
Lizzie:	No, you dumb green puppet! He knew who had healed him. It was JESUS - the SON OF GOD. So, he came back to thank Jesus and give praise to God.
Mo:	*(slowly)* "Give Praise to God." Lizzie, that means telling God how wonderful and awesome He is - especially if He's just healed you.
Lizzie:	Yeah. But you can praise Him anytime.
Mo:	Those other nine men, Lizzie, they weren't smart. They didn't recognise Jesus. They didn't see He was the Son of God.
Lizzie:	You got that right Mo.
Mo:	So, I am not a dumb green puppet then?

Joshua

By Jacqui Stok

Part 1

Joshua, son of Nun is the hero of this story.

He trusted in God, gave God all the glory.

Moses sent Josh and eleven others to Canaan,

Out of the twelve reporting back ten were complainin'.

"There's good fruit", they said, "and honey and dairy,

But the walls are too strong and the men are too scary.

We can't defeat them, forget that idea,

We much prefer manna and walking all year."

"But wait", said Josh, "You're forgetting the promise.

God is with us, don't let them con us.

We'll beat those big guys, we'll bring home the bacon,

This time next week they'll be shakin' and quakin'."

It was Josh who remembered that it's God that we trust.

We need not be worried or anxious or fussed.

If there's one thing to remember more often than not,

It's ALWAYS TRUST GOD NO MATTER WHAT.

I can't hear you, God's people, give it all that you've got.

ALWAYS TRUST GOD NO MATTER WHAT.

Part 2

After forty years of walking, Josh was now in command.

It was time for the Israelites to take the promised land.

The walls of Jericho stood firm in their way.

But God had a plan, for Joshua to obey.

"The men", God said, "Must march around the walls,

There will be no violence, no fighting, no brawls.

The men hold their weapons, the priests hold their horns,

I know it sounds boring, just ignore all the yawns.

Do this once daily for six days of the week

It'll be on the seventh, that the Jerichonians will freak.

You'll march seven times that day and when the priests' trumpets sound

Go crazy, shout loudly, and watch the walls hit the ground."

Josh obeyed God's commands and did as he said.

It happened as promised, Jericho's people were dead

For us we must remember, whether we want to or not,

To ALWAYS OBEY GOD NO MATTER WHAT.

Once more, you will say it, in case you forgot.

ALWAYS OBEY GOD NO MATTER WHAT.

Part 3

God had one rule after Jericho was humbled.

Do not take any silver or gold from the crumble.

But Achan was greedy and pocketed the treasure

Then buried the loot in his tent to his pleasure.

Shortly after, the Israelites, at Ai, were defeated.

Joshua was devastated, the people depleted.

"Oh God", Josh cried, "Why did you allow this to happen?"

"Find Achan", replied God, "look under where he's nappin".

God was angry with Achan, his sin was not condoned.
Achan and his wife and his relatives were stoned.
God was now happy and so were the Israelites.
They went back to battle, this time beating those Ai-ites.

Now listen: confess your sins, to God when you pray.
He is faithful and forgives you and takes them away.
Remember when you do a bad thing you should not,
To ALWAYS CONFESS TO GOD NO MATTER WHAT.
To confess, did you say, all the sins that I've got?
ALWAYS CONFESS TO GOD NO MATTER WHAT.

Part 4

The news of Israel's success had reached the Amorites,
The Hittites, the Perrizites, the Hivites and the Jebusites.
They joined all their armies to fight against Israel,
With a strong united force, they were sure to prevail.

The Gibeonites, meanwhile, preferred Josh's good side.
But as Israel's neighbours, they were next to be fried.
So they pooled their ideas and came up with a plan.
To trick Josh and Israel into protecting their clan.

They loaded their donkeys with old wineskins and old sacks.
They put on old clothes and wore sandals with cracks.
They brought mouldy bread that was yucky to taste.
They told Josh they came from a far away place.

Josh fell for the trick and agreed to be friends.
Then learnt of his folly, too late to make amends.
The Gibeonites were safe but were made Israel's slaves.
Josh learnt a lesson in how a child of God behaves.

God has all the answers to the questions we've got.
We can ALWAYS TALK WITH GOD NO MATTER WHAT.
This is not a suggestion, it's a great gift we've got,
So ALWAYS TALK WITH GOD NO MATTER WHAT.

Part 5

The Amorite kings decided to take on the Gibeonites.

They united their armies, preparing for a fight of fights.

But the Gibeonites went weak at the knees, they were scared.

They called on Joshua, cos of this new treaty they shared.

So Josh and his army went off to the rescue.

On the way God said, "They will not win against you".

The Israelite army took the Amorites by surprise.

And defeated them at Gibeon and gave each other high fives.

They chased all the Amorites that had decided to bale.

God helped out by pelting some runaways with hail.

Josh told the sun to stand still during the fight.

Cos they couldn't fight their enemies in the dark of the night

God granted his wish, twas noon for twenty-four hours.

Josh knew God's might, he had trust in God's powers.

So remember, next time when you're stuck in a bad spot.

GOD'S ALWAYS IN CHARGE NO MATTER WHAT.

He can move mountains, fill valleys, fix the problems you've got.

Cos GOD IS ALWAYS IN CHARGE NO MATTER WHAT.

Part 6

Joshua assembled all the Israelites one day.

He said, "The Lord our God has something to say"

God said, "I gave a promise to father Abraham,

Of my protection, many descendants, and a great deal of land.

So I sent Moses to free you from that Pharaoh guy.

I parted the Red Sea, the sea bed was dry.

I let you survive but I drowned all the meanies.

I was using my powers, this was not work of genies.

I brought you to Canaan, the great promised land.

I defeated Jericho and Ai just as I'd planned.

I beat all the Amorites and others with funny names.

So you could live in a land with great riches and gains.

Throw all those gods of your fathers away.

And choose for yourself whom you'll serve on this day."

The people cried loudly, "We will serve the Lord".

But Joshua was hesitant, he thought his men flawed.

"You won't serve the Lord, you'll sin and rebel".

"No, No", they all cried, We'll serve our God well.

"Okay Josh replied, let's make a new promise.

To serve God all days, no matter what's upon us."

We too, must make a choice whether or not,

We'll ALWAYS SERVE GOD NO MATTER WHAT.

Let's say it together, if you mean it a lot.

We'll ALWAYS SERVE GOD NO MATTER WHAT.

So we've come to the end of this message today.

To trust God, obey God and confess when we pray.

So talk with God daily, he's loving and giving,

And choose to serve God every day that you're living.

The Baby in the Hay

By Jacqui Stok

So why are there some shepherds in the Christmas play?
They only care for smelly sheep and walk around all day.
These shepherds nearly wet their pants when angels said Hello.
So why were there scared shepherds in the Christmas play?
Why so?
These shepherds were not stupid, they heard the angels' song.
They scurried off to Bethlehem, it did not take them long.
So you'll always see the shepherds in the Christmas play,
'Cos they came to worship Jesus, the baby in the hay.

So why are there some angels in the Christmas play?
There were millions in the sky that night, they made it look like day.
They weren't there just to scare shepherds and make them quake with fear.
So why are there some angels in the Christmas play each year?
Well, the angels had Good News to tell the shepherd-men.

They told them 'bout a Saviour born, in the town of Bethlehem.
So you'll always find the angels in the Christmas play,
'Cos they bring the News of Jesus, the baby in the hay.

So why are there some wise men in the Christmas play?
These wise men, they did travel from so very far away.
They thought it cool to study stars up in the night time sky.
So why were some wise men in the Christmas play? Why? Why?
These wise men knew the new bright star would lead them to a king.
They hurried there with precious pressies, the best that they could bring.
So you'll always find the wise men in the Christmas play,
'Cos they gave gifts and praised King Jesus, the baby in the hay.

So why is a big bright star in the Christmas play?
It shone so bright, it could be seen from very far away.
Wise men knew this star was different; it was a special sign.
So why's the new bright star in the Christmas play each time?
The star was sent by God to guide the wise men on their quest.
It led them to the baby King, as it shone it's very best.

So you'll always find the big bright star in the Christmas play,
'Cos it showed the Light of Jesus, the baby in the hay.

So why was there Mary in the Christmas play?
She sits up on that donkey as Joseph leads the way.
And later, in the rusty shed, she becomes a Mum.
But why was Mary in the Christmas play? How come?
God had chosen Mary to be the special one.
To be the loving mother of Jesus, God's own Son.
So you'll always find Mary in the Christmas play,
'Cos she's the chosen Mum of Him, the baby in the hay.

So why is Baby Jesus in the Christmas play?
Do you think… could it be… God planned it all that way?
That Jesus is the Main Star at the centre of the play?
For without Him in the manger there would be no Christmas Day.

So, when you watch the Christmas play, I'll tell you what you'll see.
Jesus, who is our Saviour; He came for you and me.

A Big Adventure

Alice and Tom pulled the red canoe from the water and across the sand. Nearby, Alice's father watched them. "Remember the tide," he shouted when they stopped their tugging a few metres from the water. "But it's so hard," Tom yelled back at him, "can't you help us?" "No," came the reply, "you will be doing it by yourselves tomorrow. Keep pulling!"

The camping trip idea had been hatched a week ago. Tom and Alice walked home from school on that last day of term, wondering how to spend their school holidays. They were fairly sure their parents would agree to a camping excursion but would they allow them to go on their own? It would be fun.

Then Alice suggested the canoe. "We could paddle across the inlet to the sandy beach, camp in the bush for a few days, go on some canoeing explorations each day. And paddle back home when we've had enough."

"I'll never have enough of that kind of adventure," Tom responded.

And so they tossed a coin to decide whose parents they would ask permission from first. It would be Tom's.

The two children stepped into the sunny kitchen where Tom's mother and grandmother were sharing a pot of tea. Grannie's biscuit tin was open on the table; it was full of freshly made peanut butter bikkies. In a trice the children were seated either side of Tom's Grannie, a bikkie in each of their hands. Mum put cups of water before them. "Thanks Mrs. Nelson," said Alice.

"Well, you two. Blurt it out!" Grannie announced, "I can tell when little 'uns are up to somethin'."

So they did, not leaving out any details and even adding more as the ideas popped into their heads. The grownups sat quietly listening and then Tom's Dad came through the back door and Tom and Alice blurted it all out again. "I don't have any objections to most of that," Tom's Mum said, "What did your parents say, Alice?"

"We haven't asked them yet," answered Tom, "You and Dad won the toss."

The grownups glanced knowingly at each other. "I'm just a bit concerned about the canoe, Tom. You're not very experienced."

In the end, after both lots of parents discussed it in a meeting on Alice's family's back verandah, the children got permission and plans for the big adventure began. Mr. Brown watched them every day practice paddling in the canoe and set to teaching Tom how to steer and work as a team with Alice. "One of you must be the captain of this ship, but you both are the crew. Everyone is the crew."

Soon enough the morning of their departure came. Grannie handed Alice a large plastic container, full of bikkies. "It's a watertight container, in case it goes over the side and into the drink," she said, winking at Tom, "Swallows and Amazons, and all that!" The parents gave the children hugs and last minute instructions and watched as Tom climbed in behind Captain Alice. Mr. Brown pushed the canoe into deeper water as the children lowered the paddles and began paddling. Overhead a pelican flew along the same route. The four grownups waved furiously at the seafarers in the canoe, then laughed when they saw the pelican. "Pip will be looking out for them, for sure," said Mrs Nelson, "No worries!"

At first Tom and Alice moved the canoe gracefully through the calm water. Tom was careful not to move too suddenly, thinking of the stuff they had in the canoe with them. And he didn't want Grannie to hear of her bikkies going overboard. Right on cue Alice asked, "What's this about swallows and amazons?" "It's a book my Grannie read to me, about some kids going on a little sailing boat and camping in the woods. Her Grannie read it to her when she was a girl." Tom replied.

"Just like us," said Alice, and added, "my Nan is reading the story of 'The Famous Five' to me. They go on lots of adventures too. I suppose we could be 'The Famous Two'. Or three if you count Pelican Pip. Oops! Watch out Tom. The sea is getting rough!"

Pelican Pip

Sure enough the wind had picked up, making it hard to pull the paddles through the choppy water. Pelican Pip flew low over their heads. "Keep going kids. You're nearly halfway across the inlet," he encouraged them. The two children gripped the handles of the paddles and worked as a team, lowering and raising them in unison. Tom noticed that it made the job much easier.

"LAND AHOY!!" shouted Alice, just as Tom thought his arms would break from the paddling. But now they would still have to pull the canoe a safe distance from the water. Being the crew of a sea going vessel was hard work.

Leaving the canoe under the wispy trees near the beach, the children walked ten metres into the scrubby bush where they found a perfect camping spot. A small clearing, soft grass, and a pelican waiting for them. "Let's go fishing!" Pip urged, "I know exactly where the fish are biting." "Hey," replied Alice, "I'm the captain of this expedition. I give the orders." She gave Pip a direct stare, then said, "Let's go fishing! Pip, lead the way."

That night Tom and Alice and Pip had fish for tea. Tom arranged a circle of rocks on the beach while Alice collected twigs and sticks, placing them in the circle for a campfire. Tom had learned how to clean the guts out of the fish and scrape the scales from them. He now put the fish into the pan over the fire. They sizzled and spat in the oil. Pip ate his fish raw and whole. After tea the tent was erected in the clearing and the children hung the lantern inside. As the sun disappeared below the horizon and the darkness deepened, they snuggled into the sleeping bags. They were still too excited to sleep so they told each other stories. Stories of children in a little sailing boat. Stories of a famous five. Stories they'd heard from Nan and Grannie. And then their eyes closed, and all was quiet.

Suddenly they both stirred. "What's that noise?" Tom whispered. A soft rustling was heard. "Don't know," Alice answered.

"A pirate, come to find his buried treasure?" Suggested Tom.

"No, I'm the only pirate here. Remember? I brought my eyepatch." Alice turned on the lantern and pulled the eyepatch up from around her neck and put it over one eye. "Aaarhh!" she growled, and squeezed her cheeks together while declaring, "I was born in a pirate ship!" They both laughed, but when it was quiet again they heard the snuffling again, this time near the zipper of the door.

"It's an animal," hissed Tom. "A bear?"

A gentle whimpering, followed by a tiny high pitched bark.

"It's a puppy dog!" they both cried.

As Pirate Captain Alice cradled the pup in her arms she decided it's name would be Timmy. Like in 'The Famous Five' story. Now there was a crew of four.

Day 2 of the great adventure. A little puppy, a boy, and a girl crawl out of the tent. Peanut butter bikkies and apples for breakfast. A red canoe waiting under the wispy trees on the beach, and a big pelican coming in for a wobbly landing. "Postie!!" Pip yelled, while waddling towards the children. Tom saw the postman's satchel under Pip's wing and reached in to retrieve a letter. "It's from Mum," he said. "She wants to know how we are."

"Have another look in my bag," said Pip. "Your Mum gave me pencil, paper and envelope, so you can reply. I'll deliver it with the return post."

"The return post?" asked Alice.

"He means I have to do it right now so he can fly back with the letter," Tom explained, pointing to the postman's cap that Pip wore on his head. "He is a postie."

The letter wasn't long; only six words on the paper: 'fish, pirate, Timmy.' And signed, 'The Famous Four'. When the letter was in Pip's satchel the pelican ran, flapping and jumping along the beach, trying to get off the ground. Finally, it happened and Pip the Postie became a graceful flyer.

The friends spent the whole day exploring, by land and sea. They paddled along the shoreline, following creeks into the bush then turning back when the way became blocked. They sat in the canoe listening to the birdsongs and the splash of jumping fish. Timmy was afraid of the water, staying down in the space where their stuff had been stowed. But later in the day the puppy was perched on the bow of the canoe, barking joyfully at the little waves. A true sea-dog.

Although it had been fine sunny weather all day a fierce wind blew up as Tom and Alice pulled the canoe onto the beach. Alice looked at the sky. The clouds were scudding across from the west. Several windsurfers were still on the water nearer the town; only their colourful sails could be seen in the distance. "**Red sky at night, sailor's delight. Red sky in morning, sailor's warning**," she said. "I don't know what that means but my Dad says it when we're in the canoe."

Tom thought it meant they shouldn't have a campfire. So they ate apples and sandwiches. Timmy wolfed down two of Grannie's bikkies as well.

That evening they got in the tent early and listened to the howling wind. It made the tent shudder and sometimes pushed it right out of shape, then snapping back just as suddenly. In the middle of Tom's story of the Swallows and Amazons, Alice seized his arm and spluttered, "I think the pirate has come back!" Tom knew where this conversation was going. "Aarhh!!" he began, "I was born in a pirate ..."

The tent gave an almighty shudder and the zipper was unzipped. A head of blond curls poked through the opening, followed by the rest of the creature's torso. "Bitte, mein Windsurfer ist kaputt. Ich bin allein"

In a lull in the wind's fury Alice whispered, "An alien?" Timmy barked, twice.

"Ja, allein." The stranger replied.

"But where do you come from? What planet? Why do you look like a person?" Tom blurted out. The children pushed themselves into the far end of the tent as their alien visitor swept her hair from her face and smiled. "I forget myself to speak English. My windsurfer was blown across the water in the storm and I landed here on the beach. The sail is torn." Timmy whimpered, before scampering into the arms of the blond woman. Tom and Alice decided that if the puppy trusted this alien then they could too.

Day 3 of the great adventure. A little puppy, a boy, a girl, and a German backpacker crawl out of the tent. Leftover sandwiches, a packet of potato crisps, peanut butter bikkies and an apple for breakfast. A red canoe waiting beside a windsurfer under the wispy trees on the beach. The canoe appears to be consoling the windsurfer, whose sail is in tatters. A large pelican with a postman's cap and a satchel waddles up to the group of friends. "Was ist das? I mean, what is it?" the woman asks the children, pointing to the bird.

"He is our friend. A pelican," Alice tells her. "His name is Pip."

"Pip? That is strange. My name is also Pip!" the woman said. "I was given the name Philippa, but always called Pip".

Tom and Alice had forgotten to ask the woman's name last night. They had given her a blanket and watched as she fell asleep with Timmy nestled against her. They thought of her as 'Alien'. Hadn't she told them she was alien? Or maybe that was when their imaginations were working overtime.

At that moment Pelican Pip yelled "Postie!" which meant Tom had to get the letter in the satchel. It was from his Mum.

"What does she say?" Alice asked.

"Just confused about my short letter yesterday. What shall I write to her?"

"Four words. And signed 'The Famous Five'." Alice suggested.

Tom put pencil to paper. He wrote: "Sailor's warning, alien visitor. 'The Famous Five.'"

"She will be more confused now," he said, as they watched Pelican Pip soar into the sky above the inlet, with his satchel dangling by his side.

Alien Pip was dragging her board across the sand to the water. "I can paddle across to the town without my sail, I believe. Thank you for giving me shelter and your Grannie's bikkies." One last cuddle for Timmy, and Alien Pip was away, kneeling on the surfboard and paddling with her arms. Tom and Alice sat on the sand, watching, for a long time.

The children had made up their minds that they were getting close to having 'enough adventure'. And there were only a few bikkies and apples left in their store. It was decided that half a day of adventure was best, and with that in mind they stowed some supplies in the canoe, scooped up the puppy, and dragged the vessel into the water. Soon they were moving swiftly through the rippling waves. Tom was singing to help them paddle in unison.

"Let's go over to those rocks," Captain Alice ordered, and they changed course slightly. But as they got closer Tom spoke, "It isn't safe to get too close to ro…" He never finished the sentence because they heard an awful scrapping sound as the canoe came to a juddering stop. The children held their breath, waiting for the canoe with all passengers to sink to the depths of the ocean. It didn't happen.

Alice said, "You must save yourself. The captain will go down with her ship." Timmy immediately obeyed and jumped onto the rocks. Tom followed. "We will try to get the canoe off the rock and see if we've put a hole in it." With a lot of lifting and pushing he managed to get it free of the rocks. Timmy barked encouragingly. The canoe seemed to be still seaworthy, so Tom and the puppy boarded again and they were once more on their way.

It was fun to explore the coast. Sometimes they put in at a cove and explored the beach and pools. Alice collected shells and colourful flowers. Tom found a gnarled and twisted stick of driftwood. "I'm going to paint eyes on it, and it will be a snake," he said. When the sun was high in the sky they climbed into the canoe and paddled back to their camping spot. Pelican Pip was waiting for them.

"It's well and truly lunchtime!" he told the children. Alice got the campfire going while Tom cleaned the fish Pip had caught. The last of their food was laid out and the smell of frying fish made their mouths water.

"We've had the best adventure," Tom mumbled, as he ate his lunch. Alice nodded in agreement.

It didn't take long to break camp. Everything was tucked into the storage spaces, the campfire was doused, Grannie's empty bikkie container stowed below deck. Three of the Famous Four got in the canoe and set off for home. The fourth member of the gang flew above them.

On the town beach seven people were waiting to welcome them home - all their parents, Nan, Grannie, and Alien Pip. Another grownup stood nearby but he wasn't known to the children. However, Timmy knew him! The little puppy launched himself into the shallow water and raced past the other adults to the man who called out joyfully, "Oh Matey! I thought I'd never see you again!" Alice smiled at Tom, "I always knew he was a great sea-dog."

After that there was only time for hugs and stories. New stories newly made. Of pirates, fish, a puppy, a visitor from foreign parts. Of a trusty vessel with a scraped bottom, and a faithful Postie. Of a shuddering tent in a dark stormy night. And the rhythm of paddles splashing and rising.

(The author acknowledges the works of Arthur Ransome and Enid Blyton, referenced in this story)

Eliab, The Boy Who Couldn't Be Still

Reimagining Nehemiah 8 and Psalm 8

Eliab blames his feet when they won't stop moving. He tells his mother that his legs want to dance after she asks him to stand still. "I'm trying Pa," he says to his father when he's told to stop wriggling. His middle, his tummy, his arms and elbows, they won't listen.

Then one day…

The people of God, that blessed collection of leftovers who have been rebuilding the city of Jerusalem, begin to make their way to the square before the Watergate.

Eliab skips and runs around his parents as they join the throng.

Ezra the priest stands on the platform. He lifts his arms high and praises God. Everyone does the same. Now Eliab is not the only one dancing and jumping, they're all doing it. "Amen! Amen!" They shout.

The priest begins to read. Grandpas, grandmas, mums and dads, uncles, aunties, sisters, brothers - they're all quiet and attentive. Eliab is listening but he is moving too. His feet are telling him to jump, his belly is wanting to twist, and his knees... oh, his knees are bouncy!

The holy man speaks loud and clear. His eyes look at the words of The Law on the scroll, and then his voice booms across the heads of the people. But sometimes his voice is different, it's gentle, like when he is reading a story: "If a man's donkey falls in the well…"

Sometimes he crouches down. Sometimes he waves his arms wildly. Sometimes he thumps both fists down on the lectern!

Eliab is jumping faster as he copies the priest's actions: makes himself small, swings his arms around, thumps his imaginary lectern.

Then he watches the Levite priests walk among the crowd. They are gathering people into groups. "Stand in a circle and one of us will explain the Law to you," they say. Pa tries to hold Eliab in front of him by encircling his arms around his son.

The boy who couldn't be still also likes circles; he begins tracing his finger in circles on his father's hand. It earns him 'a look'. But then their priest-teacher says something interesting and it seems to Eliab that his finger-tracing is helping him understand. As he thinks about the words he notices low, sad sounds beginning to wrap around his head.

Soon the sorrowful noise gets louder. Everyone is bowed down, bent in the middle. They are wailing with grief because of their guilt, which they've only just now discovered and understood. Eliab puts his hands over his ears and stamps his feet. Sorrow is like a heavy weight on his young shoulders. He knows he couldn't possibly be as good as the Law tells him he should be. Will God punish him? Tears fall, and the sadness is almost enough to stop him moving.

Nehemiah and Ezra go up on the platform, calling out to calm the people with comforting words. "This is the day of the LORD your God. Stop your grieving."

Eliab looks about him as people stand upright once more and hug their neighbours. They wipe their eyes and smile. Not weak little smiles but wide grins, spreading across every face.

Oh, this is too wonderful, he thinks. This joy can only come from God himself.

Suddenly he feels a mighty strength come into his limbs. Eliab's legs want him to dance, to skip, to jump, to wiggle. His arms reach up to the sky.

The priest shouts over the crowd, telling everyone to prepare for a celebration feast.

And a young lad skips in circles around his parents.

Thank you, Lord, for the young.

In ways we cannot fully grasp you have ordained them for your praise. With their busy bodies they glorify their maker. Because you know them intimately you have given each one a growing understanding and knowledge of yourself.

May we be your instruments in their lives, to nurture and encourage.

Amen.

Index of Biblical references

Genesis 15:18	Stargazing (Play)
Exodus 12	Rachel's Lamb
Numbers 21	Ellie and the Pretend Snake
Joshua	Joshua (Poem)
Nehemiah 8	Eliab, The Boy Who Couldn't Be Still
1 Samuel 1-3	Samuel – Answer to my Prayer
1 Samuel 16:1-13	David
1 Samuel 20	David and Jonathan – Friends (Play)
Psalm 139	God is my Maker (Play)
Jeremiah 38	Mud – The Story of Jeremiah (Play)
Ezekiel 4	The Man on the Ground
Zephaniah 3:17	Is God Grumpy? (Play)
Matthew 2: 1-12	Melchior, Balthazar and Caspar
Matthew 1&2	The Baby in the Hay (Poem)
Matthew 5: 44	Time for Revenge (Play)
Matthew 7: 24-27	Two Chippies
Matthew 8: 5-13	I've heard about Jesus…
Matthew 8: 28-34	Encountering Jesus

Matthew 9: 9-11	The Littlest Disciple
Matthew 12: 1-14	The Invisible Man
Matthew 13: 31,32	The Weeniest, Teeniest Seed (Play)
Matthew 18	A Child in their Midst
Matthew 26: 31-75	Honesty (Play)
Mark 6: 30-44	Feeding of the 5000
Mark 9	A Child in their Midst
Mark 14: 29-72	Honesty (Play)
Luke 2	The Baby in the Hay (Poem)
Luke 2: 41-52	Hiding
Luke 6: 46-49	Two Chippies
Luke 9	Feeding the 5000
Luke 14 & 15	The Parable of the Lost Lego Block
Luke 17: 11 – 19	Do You Recognise Me? (Play)
Luke 18: 15- 17	Stephanie's in Heaven
Luke 22: 33-66	Honesty (Play)
John 2: 1-11	The Wedding at Cana
John 2: 13-16	Jesus Clears the Temple
John 6: 1-13	Story for Rohan
John 11: 25,26	Tom's Fishing Lesson

John 13: 1-17	Telling Bible Stories to Young Children
John 18: 15-27	Honesty (Play)
Acts 6:8-7:60	The Conscript
Acts 9:1-31	Saul on the Road to Damascus (Poem)
Acts 16: 13-15	Nice (Play)
Acts 20: 20-24	God Takes the Shakes Away (Play)
2 Corinthians 5: 17	Old Martha
1 Thess. 5: 16-18	Put a Smile on God's Face (Play)
Revelation	Sophia's Pictures

www.ingramcontent.com/pod-product-compliance
Lightning Source LLC
Chambersburg PA
CBHW060521010526
44107CB00060B/2648